Janice VanCleave's

A+
PROJECTS IN
CHEMISTRY
Winning Experiments for
Science Fairs and Extra Credit

John Wiley & Sons, Inc.
NEW YORK · CHICHESTER · BRISBANE · TORONTO · SINGAPORE

Library of Congress Cataloging-in-Publication Data

Vancleave, Janice Pratt.
    Janice Vancleave's A+ projects in chemistry : winning experiments for science
fairs and extra credit.
        p.   cm.
    Includes index.
    Summary: Provides step-by-step instructions for thirty advanced chemistry ex-
periments suitable for science fairs.
    ISBN 0-471-58631-5—ISBN 0-471-58630-7 (pbk)
        1. Chemistry—Experiments—Juvenile literature. [1. Chemistry—
Experiments. 2. Experiments. 3. Science projects.] I. Title. II. Title: A+
projects in chemistry. III. Title: Janice Vancleave's A plus projects in chemistry.
QD38.V37   1994
540′.78—dc20   93-10588

It is my pleasure to dedicate this book to
a very special friend who has contributed to
positive changes in my life,
Cullen James Rogers.

Contents

Introduction

Science is a search for answers to all kinds of interesting questions about our world. Science projects make excellent tools for you to use as you look for the answers to specific problems. This book will give you guidance and provide A+ project ideas. An A+ idea is not a guarantee that you will receive an A+ on your project. You must do your part by planning experiments, finding and recording information related to a problem, and organizing the data to find its answer.

Sharing your findings by presenting your project at science fairs will be a rewarding experience if you have properly prepared the exhibit. Trying to assemble a project overnight usually results in frustration, and you cheat yourself out of the fun of being a science detective. Solving a scientific mystery, like solving a detective mystery, requires that you plan well and carefully collect facts.

Start your project with curiosity and a desire to learn something new. Then, proceed with purpose and a determination to solve the problem. It is likely that your scientific quest will end with some interesting answers.

Select a Topic

The 30 topics in this book suggest many possible problems to solve. Each topic has one "cookbook" experiment—follow the recipe, and the result is guaranteed. Read all of these easy experiments before choosing the topic you like best and want to know more about. Regardless of the problem you choose to solve, your discoveries will make you more knowledgeable about chemistry.

Each of the 30 sample projects begins with a brief summary of topics to be studied and objectives to be determined. Information relevant to the project is also included in the opening summary. Terms are defined when first used, but definitions are not repeated throughout the text. Check the Glossary and/or Index to find explanations about any terms that are unfamiliar to you.

Try New Approaches

Following each of the 30 introductory experiments is a section titled "Try New Approaches" that provides additional questions about the problem presented. By making small changes to some part of the sample experiment, new results are achieved. Think about why these new results might have happened.

Design Your Own Experiment

In each chapter, the section titled "Design Your Own Experiment" allows you to create experiments to solve the questions asked in "Try New Approaches." Your own experiment should follow the sample experiment's format and include a single purpose or statement; a list of necessary materials; a detailed step-by-step procedure; written results with diagrams, graphs, and charts, if they seem helpful; and a conclusion explaining why you got the results you did and answering the question you posed to yourself. To clarify your answer, include any information you found through research. When you design your own experiment, make sure to get adult approval if supplies or procedures other than those given in this book are used.

Get the Facts

Read about your topic in many books and magazines. You are more likely to have a successful project if you are well informed about the topic. For each topic in this book, the section titled "Get the Facts" provides some tips to guide you to specific sources of information. Keep a journal to record all the information you find from each source including the author's name, the title of the book or article, the numbers of the pages you read, the publisher's name, the city of publication, and the year of publication.

Keep a Journal

Purchase a bound notebook to serve as your journal. Write in it everything relating to the project. It should contain your original ideas as well as ideas you get from books or from people like teachers and scientists. It should also include descriptions of your experiments as well as diagrams, photographs, and written observations of all your results.

Every entry should be as neat as possible and dated. A neat, orderly journal provides a complete and accurate record of your project from start to finish and can be used to write your project report. It is also proof of the time you spent sleuthing out the answers to the scientific mystery you undertook to solve, and you will want to display the journal with your completed project.

Use the Scientific Method

Each project idea in this book will provide foundation material to guide you in planning what could be a prize-winning project. With your topic in mind and some background information, you are ready to demonstrate a scientific principle or to solve a scientific problem via the **scientific method**. This method of scientifically finding answers involves the following steps: purpose, hypothesis, research, experimentation, and conclusion.

Research: The process of collecting information about the topic being studied. It is listed as a first step because some research must be done first to formulate the purpose and hypothesis and then to explain experimental results.

Purpose: A statement that expresses the problem or question for which you are seeking resolution. You must have some knowledge about a topic before you can formulate a question that can lead to problem-solving experimentation. Thus, some research is necessary for this step, and you can find much of the information about each topic in this book.

Hypothesis: A guess about the answer to the problem based on knowledge and research you have before beginning the project. It is most important to write down your hypothesis before beginning the project and not to change it even if experimentation proves you wrong.

Experimentation: The process of testing your hypothesis. Safety is of utmost importance. The projects in this book are designed to encourage you to learn more about a chemical phenomenon by altering a known procedure, but only with adult supervision should you explore untested procedures.

Conclusion: A summary of the experimental results and a statement that addresses how the results relate to the purpose of the experiment. Reasons for experimental results that are contrary to the hypothesis are included.

Assemble the Display

Keep in mind that while your display represents all that you have done, it must tell the story of the project in such a way that it attracts and holds

Figure I.1

the viewer's interest. So, keep it simple. Try not to cram all your information into one place. To conserve space on the display and still exhibit all your work, keep some of the charts, graphs, pictures, and other materials in your journal instead of on the display board itself.

The actual size and shape of displays vary according to local science fair official rules. So, remember to check them out for your particular fair. Most exhibits are allowed to be 48 inches (122 cm) wide, 30 inches (76 cm) deep, and 108 inches (274 cm) high. Your display may be smaller than these maximum measurements. A three-sided backboard (see Figure I.1) is usually the best way to display your work. Wooden panels can be hinged together, but you can also use sturdy cardboard pieces taped together to form a very inexpensive, but presentable, exhibit.

A good title of eight words or less should be placed at the top of the center panel. The title should capture the theme of the project but not be the same as the problem statement. For example, suppose the problem under question is, What is the most effective of the traditionally used materials used to melt ice on roadways? An effective title might be, *The Effect of Colligative Properties on Melting Point.* The title and other headings should be neat and also large enough to be readable from a distance of about 3 feet (1 m). You can glue letters onto the backboard (buy precut letters or cut some out of construction paper), or you can stencil them for all of the titles. A short summary paragraph of about 100 words to explain the scientific principles involved is useful and can be printed under the title. Someone who has no knowledge of the topic should be able to easily understand the basic idea of the project just by reading the summary.

There are no set rules about the position of the information on the display. However, it all needs to be well organized, with the title and summary paragraph as the focal point at the top of the center panel and the remaining material placed neatly from left to right under specific headings. The headings you display will depend on how you wish to organize the information. Separate headings of "Problem," "Procedure," "Results," and "Conclusion" may be used.

Discuss the Project

The judges give points for how clearly you are able to discuss the project and explain its purpose, procedure, results, and conclusion. While the display should be organized so that it explains everything, your ability to discuss your project and answer the questions of the judges convinces them that you did the work and understand what you have done. Practice a speech in front of friends, and invite them to ask you questions. If you do not know the answer to a question, never guess or make up an answer or just say, "I do not know." Instead, say that you did not discover that answer during your research, and then offer other information that you found of interest about the project. Be proud of the project, and approach the judges with enthusiasm about your work.

1 Weather: Chemically Speaking

Weather is an important part of our lives. Your plans for the day (what you wear, where you go) may be determined by a meteorologist's weather forecast. Before making such predictions, however, a meteorologist must have an understanding of what causes and affects weather conditions.

In this project, you will study several weather events and determine the chemical nature of each. Clouds, for instance, are one of the many wonders of nature, and, in this first experiment, you will discover the mystery of their formation and disappearance. You will also look at the energy and phase changes involved in the formation of dew and frost. And the laws that determine how gases behave will be used to explain some weather conditions.

Getting Started

Purpose: To determine what causes clouds to form and to **dissipate** (to separate or break up).

Materials

glass soda bottle
water
candle
match
1-foot (30-cm) piece of
    aquarium tubing

modeling clay
2 or 3 books
desk lamp
masking tape
sheet of black construction
    paper

Procedure

1. Rinse the inside of the soda bottle with water.

2. Pour the water out of the bottle, leaving only enough to cover the bottom of the bottle.

3. Light the candle with the match and allow the candle to burn for 30 seconds.

4. Blow out the candle and hold the smoking wick inside the bottle just long enough for a small puff of smoke to enter it.

5. Insert about 4 inches (10 cm) of one end of the tubing into the middle of the bottle's mouth.

6. Use modeling clay around the tubing to seal off the mouth of the bottle.

7. Stack the books on a table that is next to a wall.

8. Set the bottle on the stack of books and position the lamp so that it illuminates the bottle from behind but does not shine directly in your eyes.

9. Tape the black paper to the wall behind the bottle so that it creates a dark background (see Figure 1.1).

10. Blow hard into the end of the tubing.

11. Seal the end of the tubing by bending it and holding it tightly with your fingers.

12. Observe the contents of the bottle.

13. Quickly release the tubing and immediately observe the bottle's contents.

14. Repeat the procedure of blowing into the bottle and releasing the tubing several times.

Results

The contents of the bottle look clear when air is blown into the bottle, but releasing the tubing causes the inside of the bottle to look cloudy.

Why?

Molecules in a liquid constantly move around and bounce into one another. When a liquid molecule acquires enough energy to break away from the attraction of other molecules in the liquid, it escapes as vapor into the space above the liquid. This process (liquid becoming vapor) is called **evaporation** and occurs faster as the temperature increases. **Condensation** (vapor becoming liquid) is the reverse of this process and occurs faster when the temperature decreases.

In this experiment, when air is forced into the bottle, the increase in pressure causes an increase in temperature; thus, more molecules of invisible water vapor are formed. As the air rushes out, the pressure in-

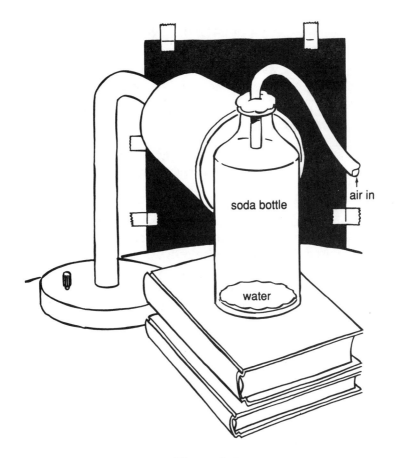

Figure 1.1

side the bottle decreases, causing the contents of the bottle to cool; thus, the water vapor changes back into liquid water.

These changes occur rapidly. Water droplets are formed as the water molecules condense and cling to the smoke particles. These droplets are large enough to scatter the light, so the bottle appears cloudy. The cloud dissipates when the water molecules vaporize. The minute smoke particles are too small to scatter the light, so the bottle appears clear.

Try New Approaches

1. Are particles in the air necessary for cloud formation? Repeat the experiment, omitting the step of adding smoke. **Science Fair Hint:** Use diagrams to compare the result of this experiment with that of the original experiment.

2. Does the amount of water affect the results? Repeat the experiment twice, first using a dry bottle, and then using twice as much water.

Design Your Own Experiment

1. Dew point is the temperature to which air must be cooled, at constant pressure, in order for it to be saturated with water. In order for **dew** (water that condenses on cool surfaces) to form, water vapor must exist in the air. The amount of water vapor is referred to as **humidity.** When the humidity is high, the dew point is also high.

Demonstrate how to measure dew point by filling a drinking glass with ice cubes and covering the ice with water. Place a thermometer in the ice water and observe the outside of the glass (see Figure 1.2). Record the temperature at which water is first observed on the outside of the glass. Repeat this experiment on days with varying humidity. You could display a diagram of the materials used and the experiment results. Include an illustration showing the energy changes necessary to make phase changes. These changes can be expressed as follows:

$$
\text{Liquid} \quad \underset{\xleftarrow{\quad - \text{ energy (condensation)} \quad}}{\xrightarrow{\quad + \text{ energy (evaporation)} \quad}} \quad \text{Vapor}
$$

2. Frost is formed when dew, formed at a temperature below 32°F (0°C), changes to ice and then grows by sublimation. **Sublimation** is the direct change from vapor to a solid and can be expressed as follows:

$$
\text{Vapor} \quad \xrightarrow{\quad - \text{ energy (sublimation)} \quad} \quad \text{Solid}
$$

Demonstrate frost formation by filling a shiny metal can half full with ice. Cover the ice with a thin layer of rock salt (ice cream salt, available at the grocery). The salt lowers the temperature of the ice water. Add more ice to fill the can and cover the ice with salt again. Pour enough water into the can to cover the ice and stir. Observe the outside of the can. Frequently, scrape your fingernail over the outside surface of the can to detect signs of frost formation. You could display photographs of the can in your project.

Get the Facts

1. Weather systems occur in the lower level of the blanket of gas surrounding the earth, which is called the *atmosphere*. To understand more about weather, you must learn more about gases. Use a chemistry text to find information about the laws that govern the behavior of gases. What are the relationships between the volume, the temperature, and the pressure of a gas? What is vapor pressure and how does it affect the relative humidity of air?

2. Frost, dew, rain, hail, sleet, and snow are all formed by increases and decreases in the temperature of water. But what determines whether the solid phase is frost, sleet, hail, or snow? Use an atmospheric science text to find out more about the conditions required to form each of these different water phases.

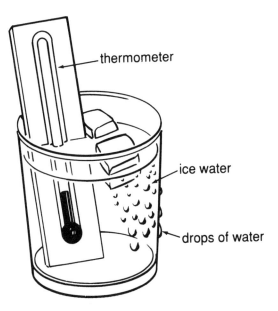

Figure 1.2   Hygrometer

3. What causes clouds to be white? Why are they more colorful in the mornings and in the evenings than at midday? The commonly accepted reason for the whiteness of clouds is the equal scattering of visible light of all wavelengths. Why then does milk look white when in fact it scatters more blue light? Find out more about colors produced by the scattering of light. What is the *Tyndall effect?*

4. Frost does not occur under cars, trees, and benches. The reason is not that these objects block falling frost as an umbrella blocks falling rain. The reason is rather that frost does not fall; it sublimes from atmospheric water vapor onto subfreezing surfaces. The absence of frost on a surface indicates that the surface, because of its *radiation energy*, is too warm for frost to form. All objects emit radiation. Find out more about heat from radiation. Why is it that only the area directly under the branches of a tree is affected by its radiant energy? How does color affect the energy of an object?

Humidity: Determined Hygroscopically

2

Hygroscopic materials absorb water from the atmosphere. Therefore, on a rainy day you may find it difficult to pour salt from a shaker unless rice has been added to the shaker to keep the salt dry.

In this project, you will use the water-absorbing property of hygroscopic materials to make a hygrometer, an instrument that measures humidity. You will study the effect of humidity on different textures of hair and various materials. You will also examine the formula for hydrated and anhydrous crystals as well as the quantity of water that different hygroscopic materials can absorb.

Getting Started

Purpose: To make and use a hair hygrometer to determine changes in the humidity of air.

Materials

ruler

scissors

4-×-10-inch (10-×-25-cm) piece
of cardboard

pencil

tissue paper

6-inch (15-cm) straight strand of
hair (not treated chemically
by perming, straightening,
and/or coloring)

glue

pushpin

marking pen

masking tape

2-liter plastic soda bottle

Procedure

1. Measure and cut out a 2-×-8-inch (5-cm×-20-cm) section from the center of the piece of cardboard.

2. Draw and cut out an arrow 2 inches (5 cm) long from the tissue paper.

3. Lay the end of the hair strand on the tip of the arrow. Place glue on a small piece of tissue paper and press it to the arrow's tip so that the end of the hair strand is sandwiched between the arrow tip and the tissue paper.

4. Use the point of the pushpin to make an enlarged hole in the blunt end of the arrow. The hole should be large enough for the arrow to rotate easily on the pin.

5. With the point of the pushpin through the hole in the arrow, insert the pin into the cardboard (see Figure 2.1).

6. Use a small piece of tissue paper with glue on it to stick the other end of the hair strand to the top of the cardboard.

7. Hold the cardboard vertically. Adjust the length of the hair strand so that the arrow hangs horizontally.

8. Mark a line on the cardboard where the arrow points to show when the arrow is level.

9. Tape the pencil to the top of the cardboard.

10. Cut off the top of the plastic soda bottle and hang the cardboard inside so that the pencil rests across the bottle and supports the cardboard.

11. Place the bottle near an open window or in a garage where outside air can reach it.

12. For two weeks, make daily observations of the position of the arrow.

13. Construct a data table such as the one shown here.

Data Table		
Date	Position of Arrow	Relative Humidity

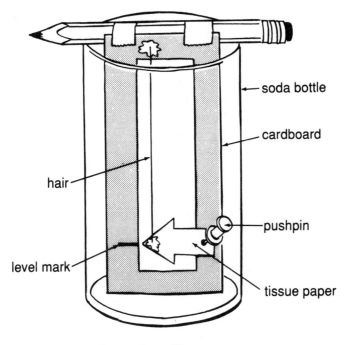

Figure 2.1   Hygrometer

a. Record a + (plus sign) when the arrow moves above the level mark and a − (minus sign) when the arrow falls below the level mark.

b. Contact the local weather bureau daily for an accurate relative humidity report.

Results

The arrow moves up when the relative humidity is low, and it moves down when the relative humidity is high.

Why?

Humidity is the amount of moisture in the atmosphere. **Relative humidity** is the measurement of how much water the air holds at a given temperature. When air holds all of the water that it can at a given temperature, it is saturated and the relative humidity is 100 percent. A **hygrometer** is used to measure changes in humidity.

Hygroscopic materials take up water vapor from the air. If the materials dissolve in the water absorbed from the air and form a solution, they are called **deliquescent**. Other materials, like the strand of hair used in this experiment, are insoluble in water but hold the water in their pores and imperfections.

The changes in the humidity of air are measured by the hair hygrometer. As the humidity increases, the hair holds more water and stretches. With a lower humidity, the hair dries and shrinks. The stretching and the shrinking of the strand of hair cause the paper arrow to move up and down.

Try New Approaches

1. Does the length of the hair strand affect the results? Repeat the experiment two times, first using a 4-inch (10-cm) strand of hair, and then using an 8-inch (20-cm) strand of hair.

2. Does color affect the hygroscopic nature of hair? Repeat the original experiment using strands of hair of different natural colors. **Science Fair Hint:** Display the hygrometer models along with the results of each test.

3. How does chemical treatment of hair such as perming, straightening, and/or coloring affect its hygroscopic property? Repeat the original experiment using a chemically treated hair sample from a beauty salon patron or from an acquaintance. Compare the distances that the arrow moves on the hygrometer made with treated hair with the distances of the arrow on the original hygrometer.

Design Your Own Experiment

1a. Do the stretching and the shrinking of hair due to its hygroscopic property change the shape of the hair strand? Hold a clean hair strand between your thumb and forefinger. Use a hair dryer to dry the strand of hair. To make the strand easier to see, hold it next to, but not touching, a sheet of paper. Use a spray bottle to very lightly mist the hair strand with water. Again hold the hair next to the paper and observe its shape. (The author's hair strand changed from a wavy shape to a spiral one.) Test different hair shapes. Do curly strands get curlier?

b. Does hair spray prevent the hair from absorbing water? Repeat this experiment using strands of hair that have been sprayed with hair

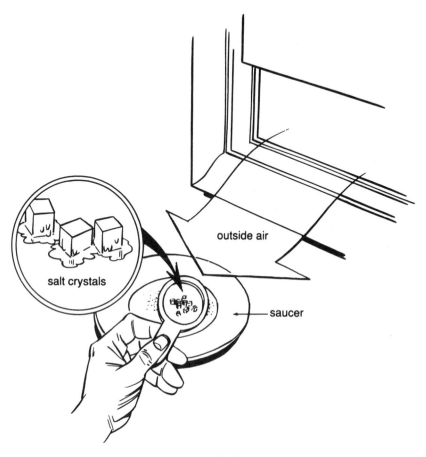

salt crystals

outside air

saucer

Figure 2.2

spray. Allow the spray to dry thoroughly about 2 minutes before mist-
ing the hair with water.

c. What is the effect of humidity on silk and wool, which, like human
hair, are hygroscopic? Repeat this experiment using silk thread and
strands of wool yarn. You could display drawings of the changes in
shape of each type of strand.

2. Sodium chloride (table salt) is deliquescent. Use this chemical to test
the humidity of the air by placing 1 tablespoon (15 ml) of salt on a
saucer near an open window so that the crystals are exposed to the
outside air (see Figure 2.2). For two weeks, use a magnifying lens to

make daily observations of the appearance of the surface of the crystals. Do changes in the relative humidity affect the appearance of the crystals?

Get the Facts

1. How much water can a deliquescent material absorb? Use a chemistry text to find out more about deliquescent materials. What is *vapor pressure*? How does the water vapor pressure of a solution and the partial pressure of water vapor in the air control the amount of water absorbed by deliquescent chemicals?

2. How do chemical formulas of hydrated chemicals differ from those of anhydrous chemicals? Use a chemistry text to find the formulas of chemicals that exist in hydrated and anhydrous forms, such as cobalt (II) chloride and copper (II) sulfate.

3 | Air: Life Supporter and Protector

The atmosphere, that thick blanket of gas enveloping the earth, provides gases necessary for the life of plants and animals. It also serves as a shield of protection from the sun's intense heat.

In this project, you will determine some of the chemical and physical properties of air. You will also look at the history of the discovery of the composition of a substance in air.

Getting Started

Purpose: To duplicate John Mayow's (1641–1679) experiment showing that burning consumes a substance in air.

Materials

modeling clay	water
candle (about half as tall as the jar used)	red food coloring
	match
cereal bowl	1-pint (500-ml) glass jar

Procedure

1. Use the clay to secure the candle to the bottom of the bowl so that the candle stands upright.

2. Fill the bowl three-fourths full with water.

3. Add drops of food coloring to make the water in the bowl a deep red.

4. Light the candle with the match. **CAUTION:** Be careful not to get your clothing or hair close to the flame.

5. Turn the jar upside down, quickly lower it over the burning candle, and stand it on the bottom of the bowl (see Figure 3.1).

6. When the flame goes out, observe the water level inside the jar.

Results

A bubble of gas escapes when the jar is placed into the water. As the candle burns, the water rises up into the jar.

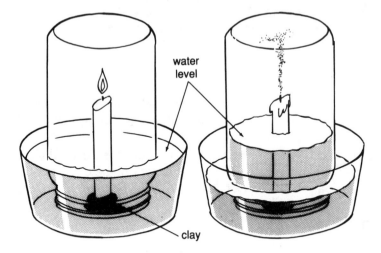

Figure 3.1

Why?

John Mayow correctly concluded that air contains a substance needed for burning. His term for this substance was "nitro-aerial spirit." His experiment, which you duplicated, was used to show that burning removed the nitro-aerial spirit from the air, leaving an empty space that was filled by the water. Mayow believed that the amount of water that rose up into the jar was equal to the amount of nitro-aerial spirit that left.

Some people still use Mayow's experiment to demonstrate that water takes the place of the oxygen that is removed as a result of the burning of the candle. If Mayow had known that heated gases expand, do you think his conclusion would have been the same? Yes, oxygen is being removed from the air, but the burning candle is producing carbon dioxide gas and water vapor. Do these gases not fill some, if not all, of the space left by the removal of elemental oxygen? These questions will be explored in the next section. Information gathered from further experimentation and research will provide you with an explanation of this experiment.

Try New Approaches

1. Does the heated air inside the jar escape, leaving a partial vacuum that is replaced by the water? Repeat the experiment using two candles sitting side by side. Quickly lower the jar over the burning can-

dles and observe the surface of the water for any bubbles that indicate a loss of air from the jar.

2a. Does the extinguished flame indicate the absence of oxygen in the jar? Could it be that carbon dioxide, which is heavier than oxygen and is produced as a result of burning the candle, forms a layer on the surface of the water? Is it the rising of this carbon dioxide layer that snuffs out the candle? Use candles of different heights to determine whether carbon dioxide affects the burning of the candle. Repeat the original experiment measuring the time the candle burns under the jar. Repeat the experiment two more times, first using a taller candle, and then using a small section of the candle placed on a 2-inch (5-cm) square piece of cardboard that floats on the surface of the water in the bowl. Compare the measured time for the burning of each candle.

b. Does the size of the jar affect the results? Repeat the original experiment two times, first using a larger jar, and then using a smaller jar.

c. Does the shape of the jar affect the results? Repeat the original experiment two times, first using a slender candle that will fit inside the neck of a glass soda bottle, and then using the same slender candle and a large-mouthed glass jar. **Science Fair Hint:** Display photographs of the bottles, jars, and candles along with the results of each test.

Design Your Own Experiment

1. A way of removing oxygen from the air without excessive heat or the production of other gases is by the **oxidation** (combination with oxygen) of a metal. This reaction can be demonstrated by the **rusting** (slow oxidation process) of iron in a steel wool pad. The reaction can be expressed as follows:

$$4Fe \ + \ 3O_2 \ \longrightarrow \ 2Fe_2O_3$$
iron plus *oxygen* yields *iron oxide*

Calibrate a 16-ounce (473-ml) glass soda bottle by placing a piece of masking tape down the side of the bottle. Add ¼-cup (63-ml) of water at a time to the bottle. Mark the height of the water after each addition until there are seven lines on the tape. Dip a piece of steel wool about the size of your fist into vinegar. **CAUTION:** Use rubber gloves to protect your hands when handling the steel wool.

With the aid of a pencil, push the wet wool into and against the bottom of the bottle. Place a drinking straw into the mouth of the bottle and use modeling clay to seal the opening around the straw. Turn the bottle upside down into a jar containing water tinted with food coloring. The end of the straw should extend below the surface of the colored water (see Figure 3.2). Observe the contents of the soda bottle after one hour.

2. Air is composed of about 78% nitrogen, 21% oxygen, 1% carbon dioxide, water vapor, and traces of **inert gases** (gases that either are unable to enter into a chemical reaction or react very slowly). This mixture of gases extends for miles (km) above the earth's surface. The weight of these gases pushes against the earth; the pressure of this weight is called **atmospheric pressure.**

Our ability to drink liquids through a straw demonstrates that air is matter in that it takes up space and has weight. Sucking on the straw removes air from the inside of the straw. The atmospheric pressure

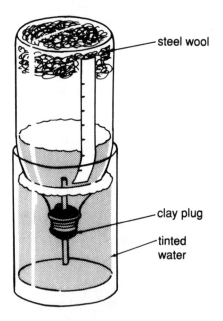

steel wool

clay plug

tinted water

Figure 3.2

pushing down on the surface of the liquid is great enough to force the liquid into the empty straw. You could use a drawing of how a straw works as part of a project display to represent one of the physical properties of air. More information about atmospheric pressure can be found in the following experiments: "Super Straw" (p. 60) and "Up and Over" (p. 68) in Janice VanCleave's *Spectacular Science Projects: Gravity* (New York: Wiley, 1992).

Get the Facts

1. The Greek philosopher Aristotle (384–322 B.C.) described the world as being made up of four elements, one of which was air. The belief that air is an element was widely held until the seventeenth century. In about 1620, the Belgian alchemist Jan Baptista van Helmont began to suspect that air was not a uniform substance; it was he who coined the word "gas." Around 1670, John Mayow conducted his experiments and concluded that a "nitro-aerial spirit" present in air was needed for burning and breathing. Find out more about these scientists and their ideas and experiments that led to the discovery that air is a mixture of oxygen, nitrogen, water vapor, and carbon dioxide with traces of inert gases. Explain Johann Becher's *terra pinguis* theory and Georg Stahl's *phlogiston theory*. What famous discovery was made by the British minister and amateur chemist Joseph Priestley? What were Antoine Lavoisier's and William Ramsay's contributions to the truth about the composition of air?

2. The atmospheric layer surrounding the earth reaches out for hundreds of miles (km). The layer closest to the earth's surface is called the *troposphere,* and it alone contains water vapor and enough oxygen to sustain life as we know it. Use an earth science text to obtain more information about the atmosphere. What are the names of the five different layers? How thick is each layer and what happens in each? How does the atmosphere control the temperature of the earth? How does the atmosphere block the sun's rays?

Biochemistry: Reactions in Living Things

4

Advertisements for soap and detergents usually stop just short of proclaiming these products to be magical.

In this project, you will analyze the chemistry behind these miracle-workers-in-a-box. You will examine the differences between soap and detergent and determine the special cleaning abilities of detergents with added enzymes. You will also look at the specialization of enzymes and their lock-and-key action.

Getting Started

Purpose: To determine the effect that the enzymes found in detergents have on protein molecules.

Materials

2 1-quart (1-liter) glass jars

water

powdered laundry detergent without enzymes

large spoon

marking pen

masking tape

powdered laundry detergent with enzymes

2 eggs (fresh, hard-boiled, and peeled)

magnifying lens

CAUTION: Always wash your hands after touching an uncooked egg. It may contain harmful bacteria.

Procedure

1. Fill the two jars three-fourths full with tap water.

2. Add 1 tablespoon (15 ml) of the laundry detergent without enzymes to one jar of water and stir.

3. With the marking pen, write "ordinary" on a piece of masking tape and tape this label to the jar.

4. Add 1 tablespoon (15 ml) of the laundry detergent with enzymes to the second jar of water and stir.

5. Label this jar "biological."

25

jar

ORDINARY   BIOLOGICAL

fresh hard-boiled egg
with shell removed

Figure 4.1

6. Place one egg into each jar.

7. Stand the jars in a warm area.

8. For 14 days, make daily observations of the surface of the eggs. Each day, lift the eggs out of the jars with the large spoon and use the magnifying lens for close-up inspection.

9. Each day, replace the eggs in a fresh solution of the appropriate mixture of laundry detergent and water.

Results

After several days, the surface of the egg in the biological laundry detergent begins to look rough, whereas the egg in the ordinary detergent remains smooth. At the end of the observation period, the egg in the ordinary detergent still looks as smooth as it did originally but the other egg has large craters in its surface. (See Figure 4.1.)

Why?

Proteins are large molecules composed of chains of smaller molecules. Each long protein molecule folds and wraps and twists back and forth on itself again and again. When the tangled strings of some proteins get

Figure 4.2

wrapped around the fibers in clothes, they cause stains. For these stains to be removed, the proteins must be broken into smaller pieces.

Enzymes, like those in the detergent used in this experiment, are biological **catalysts** (chemicals that change the rate of a chemical reaction without being changed themselves) that can be extracted from microorganisms such as bacteria. They cut the long polymer strands of proteins (as they did on the surface of the egg) without affecting the cloth fibers. The smaller molecules slip out of the cloth and are washed away with the dirt. **Science Fair Hint:** Display a drawing of this process, using scissors to symbolize an enzyme snipping off pieces of long protein strands (see Figure 4.2).

Try New Approaches

1. Does temperature affect the results? Repeat the experiment twice, first using cold water and placing the jars in a refrigerator, and then using warm water and replacing the jars with thermos bottles.

2. Does the concentration of the laundry detergent affect the results? Repeat the original experiment twice, first using 1 teaspoon (5 ml) of laundry detergent in each jar, and then using 3 tablespoons (45 ml) of laundry detergent in each jar. Compare the results of reducing the concentration by one-third with those of tripling the concentration.

3. Enzymes are biological catalysts and as such are not themselves consumed in the reaction. Can the same enzyme be used over again? Re-

peat the original experiment but do not change the solutions each day. Compare the results with those of the original experiment.

4. How do different laundry detergents compare in their ability to clean stains from cloth? Use 4-inch (10-cm) squares of white cotton cloth to prepare samples of stained cloth. Sample stains might be mustard, ketchup, and grass (rub the cloth pieces against the grass). Prepare three samples of each type of stain. Use a permanent marking pen to circle the stained area. Repeat the original experiment using two of the stained cloth pieces instead of the hard-boiled eggs. Keep the third cloth as a control to compare changes in the stain. **Science Fair Hint:** Use the dried cloth pieces as part of a project display.

Design Your Own Experiment

Biological laundry detergents (those with enzymes) cannot remove every protein stain because enzymes are fussy. That is, they are highly specific in their actions. Enzymes for the more common stains are used, but it would be impossible (at this time) to have a detergent that could clean every protein stain.

This specialization of enzymes also explains why grass and other plant materials containing **cellulose** (substance largely composing cell walls of plants) are digestible by cows but not by humans. The digestive system of a cow contains **cellobiase,** an enzyme specific for cellulose.

Discover more about the **biochemistry** (chemical reactions in living organisms) behind specific enzymes and the proteins they break apart. One model you could use to demonstrate the sensitivity of enzymes is the lock-and-key example. Each key fits only one lock, just as each enzyme "fits," or reacts with, only one protein.

Get the Facts

1. Soaps are sodium salts of long-chain *carboxylic acids*. Find out more about soap. What reactants are necessary for its production? How does the physical structure of soap give each molecule a double nature in that one end attracts water and the other has an affinity for oil? Include in your findings the history of soap making and recipes for making soap. With the assistance of your teacher or parent, prepare samples of soap and display your product.

2. Few people use soap for cleaning laundry. Instead, synthetic detergents are used. Find out more about the differences between the

chemical makeup of detergents and soap. Why are detergents used instead of soap for laundry, while soap is still used for bathing? Detergents have many components, such as surfactants, phosphates, sodium carbonates, processing agents, washer-protection agents, enzymes, perfumes, fabric whiteners, and carboxymethylcellulose. What function does each of these additives have? More information about soap and detergents can be found in Carl H. Snyder's *The Extraordinary Chemistry of Ordinary Things* (New York: Wiley, 1992), pp. 309–326.

3. Protein molecules are too large to penetrate the intestinal wall to enter the bloodstream. Enzymes in the human body cut these long polymer chains into bits and pieces so that they can pass into the bloodstream and be used. Use a biology text to gather more information about this digestive process. In your research, discover the differences between the molecular structures of starch and cellulose and why, even though you eat both, you can digest only one of them.

5 | Calories: Biochemical Energy

Food is a requirement for life. It is the body's fuel and is necessary for the production of the energy needed for daily activities and body maintenance.

In this project, you will experimentally determine the amount of heat energy released by different foods. You will use a simplified calorimeter, an instrument that measures the energy released when food burns, to determine food Calories (note the capital *C*). You will also look at the difference between gram calories and food Calories and compare the energy from carbohydrates, fats, and proteins.

Getting Started

Purpose: To make and use a simple calorimeter to determine the amount of food energy in a marshmallow.

Materials

4-×-10-inch (10-×-25-cm) piece of cardboard	metric measuring cup
aluminum foil	water
rubber band	½-pint (250-ml) canning jar
scissors	thermometer
modeling clay	match
cookie sheet	2 heat-resistant oven mitts
paper clip	helper
large marshmallow	timer

Procedure

1. Wrap the cardboard in aluminum foil.

2. Bend the covered cardboard to form a tube and secure it with the rubber band.

3. Cut two small notches, one across from the other, in what will be the bottom of the cardboard tube.

4. Place a walnut-size piece of clay in the center of the cookie sheet.

5. Cover the clay with a small piece of aluminum foil to protect it.

6. Straighten the paper clip, leaving a hook on one end. Stick the hooked end through the foil and into the clay so that the straight part of the wire stands vertically.

7. Position the marshmallow on top of the wire so that it is secure.

8. Use the measuring cup to pour 50 ml of water into the jar.

9. Stand the thermometer in the jar of water.

10. Read and record the initial temperature of the water.

11. With the match, ignite two or three sides of the marshmallow.

12. With your hands protected by the heat-resistant mitts, immediately stand the aluminum-covered tube over the burning marshmallow.

13. Set the jar of water on top of the tube above the burning marshmallow (see Figure 5.1).

14. Ask your helper to start the timer.

15. When the marshmallow stops burning, ask your helper to stop the timer.

16. Record the length of time the food burned.

17. Immediately stir the water very gently with the thermometer.

18. Read and record the final temperature of the water.

19. Calculate the temperature change by taking the **absolute difference** (subtracting the smaller from the larger number) between the initial and final temperatures. See Appendix 1 for a sample calculation.

20. Calculate the temperature change per unit of time by dividing the temperature change by the burning time.

21. Construct a data table such as the one shown here.

Data Table				
	Temperature			
Food Sample	Initial	Final	Change	Burning Time
marshmallow	72°F (22°C)	88°F (32°C)	16°F (10°C)	1.5 minutes

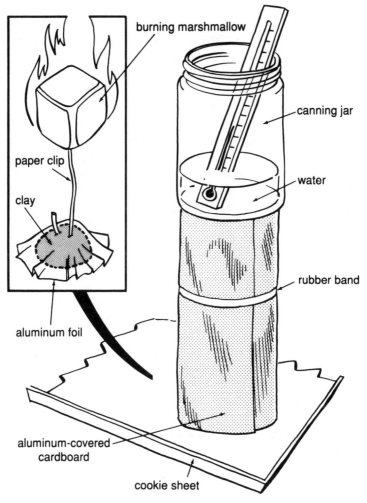

burning marshmallow

canning jar

paper clip

water

clay

rubber band

aluminum foil

aluminum-covered
cardboard

cookie sheet

Figure 5.1   Calorimeter

Results

The author's results showed a change of 16°F (10°C) in 1.5 minutes, or 10.7°F (6.7°C) per minute.

Why?

Burning is a process by which oxygen combines with a substance and **energy** (ability to do work) is released. The burning marshmallow produces **heat** (a form of energy), which is indicated by the warming of the water. Animals are dependent upon internally generated heat, which is produced by a much slower "burning" process called **respiration**. In this chemical reaction, glucose combines with oxygen to produce energy. All foods can supply the body with energy. A **calorimeter** is used to measure the energy released when food burns.

The common unit of measuring energy is the **calorie**. A **gram calorie** (spelled with a lowercase c) is the amount of heat energy required to raise the temperature of one gram of water one degree Celsius. A **food Calorie** (spelled with a capital C) is the amount of heat needed to increase the temperature of 1,000 grams of water one degree Celsius. One food Calorie is equal to 1,000 gram calories. The food Calories of energy released during the burning of the marshmallow are absorbed by the water, thus raising the water's temperature.

Try New Approaches

Is the same amount of energy per minute of time released from all foods? Repeat the experiment replacing the marshmallow with different foods, such as a peanut, cheese, and bread. **Science Fair Hint:** Construct and display a bar graph indicating the amount of energy released by each food.

Design Your Own Experiment

1. Use the following steps to calculate the amount of food Calories released by each of the burning foods. See Appendix 2 for a food Calorie sample problem.

  a. Calculate the gram calories released:

gram calories = mass of water × specific heat × temperature change

Consider the following facts:

  ▪ The **specific heat** of water is a constant equal to 1 cal/g·°C (calories needed to raise the temperature one gram of water one degree Celsius).
  ▪ The 50 ml of water weighs 50 grams, since the density of water is 1 g/ml.

b. Convert gram calories to food Calories:

$$\text{food Calories} = \frac{\text{gram calories}}{1,000}$$

2. The food used in each experiment is not totally burned. To determine the number of grams of each food sample converted into energy, divide the number of food Calories per gram into the number of food Calories absorbed by the water. A list of food Calories per gram for different foods can be found in a nutrition text.

3. The human body uses energy through exercise; **specific dynamic action,** or **SDA** (digesting and metabolizing food and converting it into energy); and **basal metabolism** (all the work that goes on inside the body to keep it alive). Energy taken into the body equals energy used plus stored energy. This relationship can be expressed as follows:

energy input = energy output + energy stored

Energy input is the amount of food Calories eaten. Energy output is the energy expended through exercise, SDA and basal metabolism. The unused energy is stored as body fat. SDA is equal to about 10% of your food energy input, and basal metabolism is roughly one food Calorie per hour per kilogram of body weight.

Determine your energy input during a 24-hour period by recording your food intake and using a calorie counter, which can be found in a nutrition text, to determine the food Calories for each food quantity. Record the total food Calories in a data table such as the one shown on the next page. Keep a record of the time duration of each physical activity during the 24-hour period and, with the Calorie counter information found in Appendix 3, calculate and record your exercise calories for the testing period. Calculate your SDA and basal metabolism.

The total results for one test subject are listed in the data table here. Sample calculations for determining these food Calories, exercise calories, SDA, and basal metabolism are provided in Appendix 4. More information about energy input and output can be found in Carl H. Snyder's *The Extraordinary Chemistry of Ordinary Things* (New York: Wiley, 1992), pp. 341–344.

Data Table for Test Subject		
	Energy Input	= Energy Output + Energy Stored
Date	Food (Calories) Eaten	Exercise + SDA + Basal + Stored
Total	5000 C	= 2,315C + 500C + 1,632C + 5,53C

Get the Facts

1. The number of food Calories in food is determined by a *bomb calorimeter.* Use a nutrition text to find out how this instrument works.

2. The *first law of thermodynamics* states that energy is not created or destroyed. Energy is just changed from one form to another, as it was in the original experiment. In the formation of the chemicals inside the marshmallow, energy was taken in and stored. The burning of the marshmallow released this stored energy. Chemical reactions are usually accompanied by the absorption or release of energy. Find out more about the gain and loss of energy during chemical changes. Define and provide examples of *endothermic* and *exothermic* reactions.

3. Fats yield more than twice as much energy per gram as do proteins or carbohydrates. Find out more about the energy differences of these major food components. What is the actual quantity of energy provided by each? What is adipose tissue and how much energy can it store?

6 Fatty Acids: Saturated and Unsaturated

Oils and fats are easily identified: Oils are liquid at room temperature; fats are solid. Oils may appear to be alike, but their chemical makeup can be very different.

In this project, you will experimentally differentiate between saturated and unsaturated oils. You will test the degree of unsaturation of different oils and determine the effect of temperature on the breaking of chemical bonds in unsaturated oils. You will also compare ability of saturated and unsaturated oils to flow, and determine the effect of temperature on the oils' viscosity.

Getting Started

Purpose: To test for the presence of an unsaturated oil.

Materials

2-quart (2-liter) cooking pot	eyedropper
water	tincture of iodine
metric measuring cup	spoon
safflower oil	stove
baby-food jar	timer

Procedure

CAUTION: Keep the iodine out of reach of small children. It is poisonous and is for external use only.

1. Use the measuring cup to pour 25 ml of safflower oil into the baby-food jar.
2. Use the eyedropper to add five drops of iodine to the oil. Stir with the spoon.
3. Record the time as zero and describe the contents of the jar in a data table such as the one shown on page 38.

4. Fill the pot with 2 inches (5 cm) of water and place it on the stove.

5. Stand the jar of oil in the pot.

6. Heat at a medium temperature.

7. Record an observation of the contents of the jar every two minutes for ten minutes.

8. Turn off the heat. Leave the jar in the pot of water to cool before disposing of the oil.

Data Table		
Mixture	Time (minutes)	Observation
Safflower + iodine	0	reddish brown with drops of undissolved iodine within the liquid

Results

The addition of iodine to the pale yellow oil turns it slightly reddish brown, and small drops of iodine can be seen suspended throughout the liquid. As the oil is heated, it returns to its original pale yellow color.

Why?

Oil molecules are **polymers** (large molecules containing small single molecules linked together). Fatty acids are the **monomers** (small molecules linked to form polymers) that bond with glycerol to make oil molecules. Fatty acids are made of carbon, hydrogen, and oxygen. The carbon atoms in the acids bond together. The carbons connect by one or two bonds. Molecules of oil with single bonds between the carbon atoms are said to be **saturated.** Molecules of oil with two or more double bonds are referred to as **unsaturated.** The more double bonds in a molecule, the more unsaturated it is.

In a saturated molecule, each carbon atom is connected to four atoms, as illustrated by the following ethane gas molecule:

ethane

In an unsaturated molecule, each carbon atom is connected to fewer than four other atoms. Ethene, for example, is an unsaturated molecule in which each carbon atom is connected to three atoms:

$$H - C = C - H$$
$$\quad | \quad | \quad$$
$$\quad H \quad H$$
ethene

Note: The line between each symbol represents a single bond between the atoms. The double lines represent a double bond.

In the presence of other chemicals, such as iodine, one of the multiple bonds breaks and the iodine atoms attach to the carbon atoms until four atoms are bonded to each carbon atom. In this experiment, iodine is responsible for the amber color of the tincture of iodine solution. Heating the safflower oil aids in breaking the multiple bonds between the carbon atoms. Iodine loses its color as it connects to the oil molecules.

Oils combine with iodine in proportion to the number of double bonds the oils contain. The combination of iodine with ethene provides a simple illustration of how the iodine bonds with an unsaturated molecule:

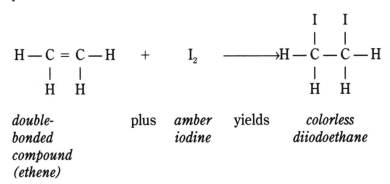

double-	plus	*amber*	yields	*colorless*
bonded		*iodine*		*diiodoethane*
compound				
(ethene)				

Try New Approaches

1. How are less saturated oils affected by iodine? Repeat the experiment replacing the safflower oil with peanut oil and comparing the results with those of the original experiment (see Figure 6.1). **Science Fair Hint:** Display colored diagrams to represent the results of the addition of iodine to saturated and unsaturated oils.

2. How does iodine affect the degree of unsaturation of different oils? Repeat the original experiment using different oils, but add the drops

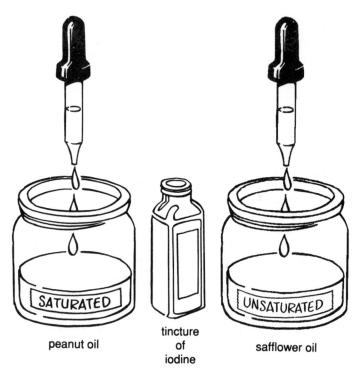

tincture
peanut oil   of   safflower oil
                   iodine

Figure 6.1

of iodine one at a time. Wait until the oil clears before adding the next drop. Continue to add the iodine until the color does not clear. To speed up the process, use a smaller container of oil such as a test tube. **Science Fair Hint:** Construct and display a bar graph comparing the number of iodine drops added to each sample of oil.

Design Your Own Experiment

1. How do low temperatures affect the way unsaturated bonds are broken? Pour 25 ml of safflower oil into two paper cups. Leave one cup at room temperature and place the second cup in a freezer. After one hour add five drops of tincture of iodine to each cup and stir. Wait five minutes and note any color changes in the cups.

2a. How does the bonding in an oil affect its **freezing point** (temperature at which it solidifies)? Fill two small paper cups with oil, one with peanut oil and the other with safflower oil. Label the cup with peanut

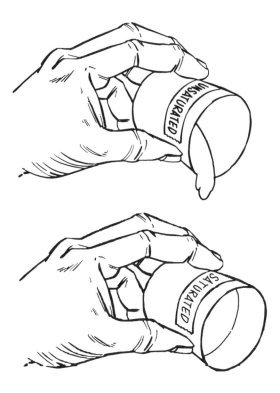

Figure 6.2

oil "Saturated" and the cup with soybean oil "Unsaturated." Tilt each cup slowly to determine the **viscosity** (resistance to flow). Place the cups in a freezer for 2 hours. Remove the cups and test the viscosity again by slowly tilting each cup (see Figure 6.2).

b. Do the oils return to their original viscosity after warming to room temperature? Allow the cups to sit on a table at room temperature. Test their viscosity by tilting each cup every 10 minutes for one half hour.

Get the Facts

1. *Triglycerides* are the main compounds in fats and oils. They are made of basic fat molecules. Each contains three molecules of fatty acid and one molecule of glycerol. Use a chemistry text to find out about the formation of triglyceride. What is the structure of glycerine, the building block of triglyceride? What are some of the fatty acids linked to glycerol? Write the reaction between glycerin and carboxylic acid molecules.

2. There is some medical evidence that saturated fats cause deposits to form in blood vessels, thus reducing the blood flow. But not all fats are bad; in fact, we cannot live without some fat in our diet. Information about the amounts and types of fats needed for good health can be obtained from the American Heart Association.

3. In order for fat to be absorbed across the intestinal wall and enter the circulatory system, it must be broken down chemically into smaller molecules. Use a biology text to find out about this *emulsification* process.

4. The amount of iodine that will combine with fatty acids in fat molecules depends on the number of double bonds the fat molecules contain. Use a nutrition text to find information about the *iodine number.* You could display a chart listing the common fats and oils and their iodine numbers.

Vitamin C Content: Analysis of Food by Titration

7

Vitamin C is required for good health. This vitamin is not produced by your body and must be obtained from foods or vitamin tablets.

In this project, you will use the titration method to determine the amount of vitamin C in various foods and vitamin tablets. You will also determine whether fruit drinks and fruit juices have comparable amounts of vitamin C. Vitamin C's antioxidant properties will be studied, and its part in an oxidation-reduction reaction will be examined. You will also look at the sources and uses of different vitamins.

Getting Started

Purpose: To determine the amount of iodine needed to react with a standard solution (carefully measured quantity) of vitamin C.

CAUTION: Be careful not to allow the vitamin C to touch your skin, in case you have any sensitivity to the chemical.

Materials

100-mg ascorbic acid (vitamin C) tablet

wax paper

hammer

½ cup (125 ml) of distilled water

1-quart (1-liter) jar

spoon

4 baby-food jars

marking pen

masking tape

1-teaspoon (5-ml) measuring spoon

starch solution (see Appendix 5)

sheet of white paper

eyedropper

tincture of iodine

Procedure

CAUTION: Keep the iodine out of reach of small children. It is poison-ous and is for external use only.

1. Prepare a standard vitamin C solution by:
- crushing the vitamin C tablet (place it between two sheets of wax paper and hit it gently with a hammer).
- pouring ½ cup (125 ml) of distilled water into the quart (liter) jar.
- adding the crushed vitamin C powder to the water in the jar.
- stirring until the powder dissolves.

2. Pour equal portions of the standard vitamin C solution into four baby-food jars.

3. With the marking pen, write "A," "B," "C," and "D" on pieces of mask-ing tape and tape one label to each jar.

4. Add 1 teaspoon (5 ml) of the starch solution to each jar.

5. Place jar A on the sheet of white paper.

6. Fill the eyedropper with tincture of iodine. Slowly add the iodine in the eyedropper to jar A, counting each drop added (see Figure 7.1). Swirl the jar after each addition of five drops. Continue to add the io-dine until the jar's contents remain a blue-black color.

7. Record the number of drops required to turn the jar's contents this blue-black color.

8. Repeat the procedure using jars B, C, and D.

9. Add the results for the four jars and divide by four to compute the av-erage number of drops of iodine needed to react with the 25 mg of vi-tamin C in each jar. *Note:* This number will be used to calculate the concentration of vitamin C in other substances.

Results

The vitamin C-starch solution is unaffected by the initial drops of iodine, but adding more iodine results in a blue-black solution. *Note:* The number of drops of iodine needed to react with the 25 mg of vitamin C in the solution will vary with the size of the eyedropper.

Why?

Titration is the process of combining a measured amount of a solution of known concentration with a measured amount of solution of unknown

Figure 7.1

concentration. Tincture of iodine is a mixture of elemental iodine (I_2) and ethyl alcohol (C_2H_5OH). The combination of elemental iodine and vitamin C chemically changes vitamin C (ascorbic acid) to a compound ineffective as a vitamin called **dehydroascorbic acid.** The elemental iodine is changed to a charged particle called **iodide** (I^-).

Elemental iodine reacts with starch to produce a blue-black color, but mixing the charged particle iodide with starch does not produce a color change. When starch, vitamin C, and elemental iodine are mixed, the iodine is more attracted to the vitamin C molecules. The starch stays in the solution unchanged until all of the vitamin C has combined with the elemental iodine. When the last molecule of vitamin C reacts with the iodine, then the starch molecules combine with any remaining iodine, producing a starch-and-iodine, blue-black–colored complex molecule.

Try New Approaches

1. Analyze a multiple-vitamin tablet to determine the amount of vitamin C in it. Repeat the experiment substituting a multiple-vitamin tablet for the vitamin C tablet. *Note:* Avoid using a multiple vitamin that contains vitamin E, which may affect the results.

The number of drops of iodine needed to react with the vitamin C mixture depends on the size of the drops, which is determined by the eyedropper. Thus, the same size eyedropper must be used throughout the experiment. Use the following equation and the known number of drops of iodine required to react with 25 mg of vitamin C to compute the amount of vitamin C in the test material (the multiple-vitamin tablet). See Appendix 6 for an example calculation.

$$\frac{\text{mg of vitamin C in test solution}}{\text{drops of iodine}} = \frac{25 \text{ mg of vitamin C}}{\text{drops of iodine}}$$

2. Determine the concentration of vitamin C in citrus fruit juices. Repeat the original experiment replacing the vitamin C solution with ½ cup (125 ml) of each fruit juice to be tested. If the juices contain pulp, strain them through cheesecloth before beginning the experiment. Again, use the equation comparing the drops of iodine needed to react with 25 mg of vitamin C to calculate the number of milligrams of the vitamin in each sample of fruit juice.

3. Does temperature affect the concentration of vitamin C? Repeat the original experiment twice, first substituting 25 ml of boiled orange juice for the standard vitamin C solution, and then using ½ cup (125 ml) of frozen orange juice that has been thawed. Use the equation again to compute the amount of vitamin C in the test solution.

4. Does storing orange juice in an open container affect the vitamin C content? Repeat the original experiment using 2 cups (500 ml) of orange juice prepared by diluting a small can of frozen orange juice according to the directions on the container. Pour 1 cup (250 ml) of orange juice into two separate jars. Place a lid on one container. Each day, test a ⅛ cup (31 ml) sample from each container.

Design Your Own Experiment

In the analysis experiments for vitamin C content, the vitamin C acts as a **reducing agent** (causes other chemicals to gain electrons). As a reducing agent, vitamin C is readily oxidized itself and therefore prevents other

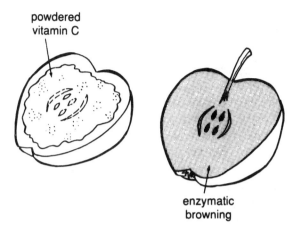

powdered
vitamin C

enzymatic
browning

Figure 7.2

chemicals from being oxidized. A chemical that undergoes oxidation has gained oxygen and/or lost electrons. You will study more about the **redox** (oxidation-reduction) reaction under "Get the Facts."

Apples contain enzymes that speed surface browning where the surface is exposed to the oxygen in the air. Vitamin C prevents this "enzymatic browning" due to oxidation of the fruit. To demonstrate vitamin C's antioxidation abilities, cut an apple in half (see Figure 7.2). Crush a vitamin C tablet and sprinkle it on one of the apple pieces. Allow the apple to sit uncovered and make observations every hour for three hours.

The antioxidant property of fruit juices and drinks can give an indication of their vitamin C content. Dip cut pieces of apple into several testing solutions and allow each piece to sit uncovered. Describe the appearance of the apple pieces immediately and then every hour for three hours. Rate the vitamin C content of the testing solutions by degree of enzymatic browning. Record the results in a data table such as shown here.

Data Table for Enzymatic Browning of Apples				
	Time (hours)			
Testing Liquid	0	1	2	3
apple juice				
lemonade				

Get the Facts

1. Vitamins contain a variety of complex chemicals. Like ascorbic acid (vitamin C), vitamins have names but are frequently identified by letters, such as A, B, C, D, E, and K. How all vitamins are used by the body is not exactly known, but we do know that many chemical reactions cannot occur in the human body if the proper vitamins are missing. For example, for calcium and phosphorous to be effective in the formation of teeth, vitamin D must be present. Use chemistry and biology texts to find out more about the uses of vitamins. Are chemists, such as Linus Pauling, correct about the role of vitamin C in helping to prevent colds? Is there any evidence to substantiate Pauling's views about the vitamin? What chemical reactions is vitamin C known to be involved in that keep your body functioning normally? What effect does the lack of individual vitamins have on the human body?

2. When skin is exposed to sunlight (ultraviolet rays), *cholesterol* (a fat-related compound) is chemically converted to vitamin D. Fresh citrus fruits are a good source of vitamin C. Find out more about the natural sources of vitamins. How have the refining and the processing of foods affected their vitamin content?

3. The titration method was used in this project to determine an unknown concentration of vitamin C. Find out more about this process. Use a chemistry text to find the meaning of the following terms: *titration, end point, indicator,* and *standard solution.* You could use this information when preparing an oral presentation and a written report.

4. Combining vitamin C and tincture of iodine results in a redox reaction in which ascorbic acid is oxidized and iodine is reduced. Find out more about the following terms: *redox reaction, oxidized, reduced, oxidizing agent,* and *reducing agent.* What is the difference between the structure of vitamin C (ascorbic acid) molecules and the structure of dehydroascorbic acid, into which the vitamin C is changed as a result of the redox reaction?

Minerals: Chemicals Needed for Life and Good Health

8

Food minerals are required for life and good health. They consist of inorganic (compounds without carbon and hydrogen) salts and are found in the foods you eat.

In this project, you will examine the functions of different food minerals and their effect on the human body. You will learn about the deposition and growth of calcium crystals within the body and demonstrate reverse calcification of a bone. You will also look at the effect of mineral ion concentration inside and outside body cells.

Getting Started

Purpose: To demonstrate the effect of acids on bones.

Materials

steak knife

uncooked chicken leg

1-quart (1-liter) jar with lid

white vinegar

Procedure

1. Carefully cut as much of the meat away from the chicken leg bone as possible.

2. Examine the flexibility of the bone by trying to bend it with your fingers.

3. Place the cleaned bone in the jar.

CAUTION: Wash your hands after handling the chicken because uncooked chicken can be contaminated with salmonella bacteria.

4. Cover the bone with vinegar.

5. Secure the lid on the jar (see Figure 8.1)

6. After 24 hours, remove the bone from the jar and examine it for flexibility.

Figure 9.1

7. Replace the bone in the vinegar.
8. Examine the bone for flexibility each day for seven days.

Results

The flexibility of the bone increases daily. At the end of the test period, the bone feels very rubbery.

Why?

During fetal development, strong fibers of protein called **collagen** form a **matrix** (pattern) for bones. The matrix is shaped like the bones but is very flexible. The matrix solidifies by a process called **calcification.** During this process, calcium phosphate or hydroxyapatite, $Ca_{10}(PO_4)6(OH)_2$, is deposited in the fibers of collagen and gives the bones strength and rigidity.

In this experiment, soaking the bone in vinegar leaches out the calcium compounds, resulting in **reverse calcification.** The rubbery bone-shaped form that results is the original collagen "mold" for the bone.

Try New Approaches

Bacteria in your mouth chemically change some of the sugars in food into acid. This acid, like vinegar, reacts with the hydroxyapatite compound in your teeth. Does body temperature speed up the decalcification reaction? Does temperature affect the speed of the reaction between the acid and the calcium compound? Repeat the experiment two times, first storing the jar containing the vinegar and bone in a refrigerator, and then using a thermos bottle of heated vinegar. Heat the vinegar to about 100°F (38°C), pour the hot liquid into the thermos bottle, add the bone, and secure the lid. Reheat the vinegar each day.

CAUTION: Wear heat-resistant oven mitts to protect your hands when pouring the hot liquid.

Make a daily comparison of the flexibility of the bones.

Design Your Own Experiment

1. Can a decalcified bone resorb (absorb again) calcium? Soak the rubbery bone in a solution of 1 teaspoon (5 ml) of calcium oxide (pickling lime from the grocery) and 1 quart (1 liter) of water. Test the flexibility of the bone each day for seven days.
2. Malcolm Bourne, a food scientist at Cornell University, is working on a process of putting the firmness back into cooked vegetables. He lowers the cooking temperature and adds calcium to the food. Bourne claims that the calcium molecules chemically combine with the **pectin** (gluey material that binds vegetable fibers together) in the vegetable. This "salt bridge" holds the vegetable molecules together, resulting in a firmer texture.

   Blanching is the process of cooking vegetables briefly at a high temperature to drive out gases that can cause sour tastes and smells. Blanch 1 quart (1 liter) of fresh string beans by placing them in 2 quarts (2 liters) of boiling water and keeping the water at a boil for five minutes. Remove from the heat, cool, and test their crispness by bending several beans back and forth with your fingers.

   Test Bourne's blanching process by adding ½ teaspoon (2.5 ml) of calcium oxide (pickling lime) to 2 quarts (2 liters) of water. Heat the water to approximately 150°F (66°C). Place 1 quart (1 liter) of fresh string beans in the water for five minutes. Remove, cool, and test for

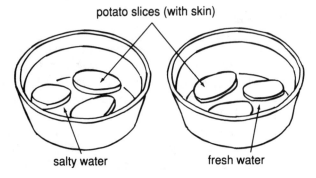

Figure 8.2

crispness as before. Compare the crispness of these beans with the crispness of the beans in the first blanching process. You could repeat the Bourne process, changing the amount of calcium oxide added to the water.

3. Sodium is the major **cation** (positive chemical particle) in **extracellular fluid** (fluid outside the cell membrane). It is responsible for keeping water in the blood from entering the cells. Potassium is the major cation inside the cell, and it keeps water from leaving the cell. When the concentration of either of these **ions** (charged particles in solution) gets out of balance, water moves into or out of cells until a new balance is achieved. The movement of water through the cell membrane is called **osmosis.**

   a. To demonstrate the effect of an increase of sodium ions in extracellular fluids, mix 1 tablespoon (15 ml) of salt in 1 cup (250 ml) of water in a small bowl. Cut three potato slices, each about ¼ inch (6 mm) thick. Check their flexibility by bending the slices back and forth with your fingers. Place the potato slices in the salty water (see Figure 8.2). After 15 minutes, test the flexibility of the potato slices again.

   b. To demonstrate the effect of an increase in minerals inside a cell, place the same potato slices in a bowl of fresh water. After 15 minutes, test the slices for flexibility as before.

Get the Facts

1. During growth and throughout adult life, bones are remodeled and reshaped. About 20% of adult bone calcium is resorbed by the body

each year. Use a nutrition text to find out more about the function of calcium in the human body. How much calcium is deposited each day in adult bones? What is the difference between the calcium compounds in teeth and those in bones? What is calcium's role in blood clotting? What function does calcium play in biological reactions such as the absorption of cobalamin (vitamin B[12])? What factors affect the absorption of calcium by the body?

2. Phosphorous is a major component of teeth and bones. Find out more about other vital roles that phosphorous plays in body functions. What is its role in the regulation of energy release? How does it affect the absorption and transportation of nutrients? How is it involved in the calcification of bones and teeth? What is the food source of phosphorous? How does a deficiency of phosphorus affect the body?

3. Find out more about other necessary body minerals such as magnesium, sodium, potassium, and chlorine. What is the function of each in the body? What is the daily requirement for each? What are the effects of too little or too much of each? What is the source of these minerals?

4. *Plaque* is the thin, adhesive polysaccharide film that covers the enamel layer of teeth. Acids that come from plaque attack the enamel and cause the calcium to be removed, as it was from the chicken bone used in this experiment. Holes form where the calcium is removed. More information about the causes of *dental caries* (tooth decay or cavities) can be provided by your dentist. How do toothpastes prevent the buildup of plaque? What is the composition of a typical *dentifrice* (toothpaste)?

9 Proteins: Changed by Denaturing

Protein molecules are vital to life. They are the molecules that provide the very shape of our bodies.

In this project, you will learn about the shape of protein molecules and the effect of their shape on their chemical behavior. You will analyze different methods of denaturing, the process by which the sizes or shapes of the protein molecules are changed. You will also look at the bonding between the protein molecules of curly hair and of straight hair and determine methods of changing the bond.

Getting Started

Purpose: To demonstrate the denaturing of gelatin (a protein) with an acid.

Materials

3-ounce (85-g) packet of
  flavored gelatin

6 3-ounce (90-ml) paper cups

refrigerator

¼ teaspoon (1.2 ml) of meat
  tenderizer

spoon

marking pen

masking tape

cereal bowl

Procedure

1. Prepare the flavored gelatin by following the instructions on the packet.
2. Pour equal amounts of the prepared gelatin into the six paper cups.
3. Place four of the cups in the refrigerator for use in later experiments.
4. Allow the two remaining cups to sit at room temperature for 30 minutes.
5. Add the meat tenderizer to one of the two remaining cups and stir well.

6. With the marking pen, write "Meat Tenderizer" on a piece of masking tape and tape this label to the cup.

7. Label the second cup "Gelatin."

8. Place the labeled cups in the refrigerator overnight (see Figure 9.1).

9. Remove the two labeled cups from the refrigerator.

10. Tilt the cups horizontally over the bowl.

11. Observe the **fluidity** (ability to flow) of the contents of each cup.

Results

The warm liquid in the cup labeled "Gelatin" changes into a semisolid, quivering mass when chilled. The gelatin containing the meat tenderizer does not become firm; it remains a liquid.

Why?

Proteins are large chains of amino acids joined together. These macromolecules often contain thousands of amino acids. The long protein molecules in the gelatin dissolve in hot water and form a **colloidal mixture** (solution with large solute molecules suspended throughout). The gelatin (protein) molecules are forced apart and are surrounded by water molecules. As the solution cools, chemical bonds form between the protein molecules. The bonds between the protein molecules produce a lattice network in which water molecules in the solution become trapped; thus, the solution "gels" into a firm, jellylike substance.

Enzymes are chemicals that cause specific chemical reactions to occur. The meat tenderizer contains an enzyme that breaks large protein molecules into smaller molecules. (When used on meat, the tenderizer thus makes the meat easier to chew.) In the gelatin, the smaller molecules formed during this **denaturing** process do not form a network of bonding; thus, the solution does not gel.

Try New Approaches

1a. Meat tenderizers contain the same enzyme that is found in fresh pineapples, or one similar to it. Repeat the experiment replacing the meat tenderizer with 1 teaspoon (5 ml) of fresh chopped pineapple.

   b. Canned pineapples are heated during the canning process. Repeat the previous experiment replacing the fresh pineapple with canned

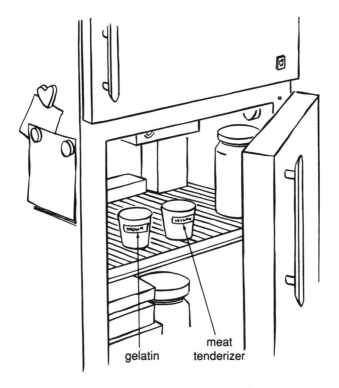

Figure 9.1

pineapple. Does heat change enzymes and cause them to not function properly?

2. Does heat affect the ability of enzymes to denature proteins? Repeat the original experiment placing the meat tenderizer in the boiling water used to prepare the gelatin. Boil the water for several minutes before adding it to the gelatin.

Design Your Own Experiment

1. Can the protein be denatured once the protein network has formed? Use the four congealed cups of gelatin made in the original experiment. Sprinkle 1 teaspoon (5 ml) of meat tenderizer on the surface of the gel in one cup; use a different brand of tenderizer in the second cup. In the third cup, place 1 teaspoon (5 ml) of chopped fresh pineapple; in the fourth cup, choose any fresh fruit, such as a banana or an

apple. Store the gelatin cups in the refrigerator overnight. Observe the surface of each cup for indications that the solid gel has liquefied.

2. Hair is made of long chains of protein molecules. These chains of molecules are called polymers. The protein molecules in hair line up, with chemical bonds connecting the molecules like steps on a ladder. There are two types of bondings that form the steps of this ladderlike structure. One bond is a connection between two sulfur atoms, one from each adjacent protein molecule. Sulfur-to-sulfur bonds are very strong. The other bond, a hydrogen bond, is weaker. In straight hair, the protein molecules lie straight, with the bonds linking them together. But in curly hair, the protein molecules are looped around, with the bonds holding them in place. To change the shape of hair, bonds have to be broken, the hair reshaped, and new bonds formed. Heat is one way of temporarily changing the hydrogen bonding in hair protein.

   a. Choose a helper with straight hair. Wrap a lock of your helper's straight hair around a heated curling iron for the amount of time indicated in the iron's instructions. Take before and after photographs of the hair for display.

   b. Choose a helper with curly hair. Straighten a lock of hair by asking your helper to hold a lock of his or her hair as straight as possible while you apply heat with a hair dryer as described in the dryer's instructions (see Figure 9.2). Again use before and after pictures to display the results.

3. A change of the hydrogen bonding in the hair protein lasts until the hair is wet; the proteins then return to their natural position. For a more permanent change, chemicals have to be used to break the sulfur bonds, the hair reshaped, and new sulfur bonds formed. A "permanent" is a procedure used to curl hair. First, a chemical is used to break the sulfur and hydrogen bonds. Then, a second chemical, the neutralizer, is used to stop the bonds from breaking and allow new bonds to form, thus holding the hair in its new shape even after wetting. Demonstrate the changes made by the chemicals of permanents by collecting samples of hair from a cosmetologist. Follow the instructions in a commercial home permanent kit to curl these hair samples.

Get the Facts

1. The term *protein* was introduced by Gerardus Mulder. This nineteenth-century Dutch chemist and physician believed that protein was

Curly   Straight

Figure 9.2

of prime importance to the functioning of the body and to life itself. Find out more about the scientist who contributed to our understanding of protein molecules' chemical composition, sources, and functions. Also look for information about Frederick Sanger's analysis of the protein called *insulin*.

2. Hydrogen bonds are not true bonds because there is no transfer or sharing of electrons. Use a chemistry text to find out more about the connection called *hydrogen bonding*.

10

Carbohydrates: Mono-, Di-, and Polysaccharides

Carbohydrates are an important source of food energy. Carbohydrates exist in foods in different forms: monosaccharides (single sugars), disaccharides (double sugars), and polysaccharides (many sugars).

In this project, you will test for the presence of the different forms of carbohydrates. Foods containing simple sugars will be identified and the amount of sugar in each compared. You will also look at differences between complex and simple sugars.

Getting Started

Purpose: To test for the presence of **monosaccharides** (simple, single molecules of sugar)—in this case, glucose and fructose.

Materials

2-quart (1-liter) cooking pot

water

stove

2 tablespoons (30 ml) of each liquid food sample: soda, diet soda, honey, apple juice

1 tablespoon (15 ml), or a pea-size sample, of each solid food sample: banana, sugar, onion, pasta

8 baby-food jars

distilled water

monosaccharide testing solution (see Appendix 5)

forceps or pot holder

Procedure

1. Prepare a water bath by filling the pot with 2 inches (5 cm) of water.

2. Place the pot of water on the stove and heat to boiling.

3. While the water is heating, prepare the food samples by placing each sample in a separate baby-food jar (see Figure 10.1).

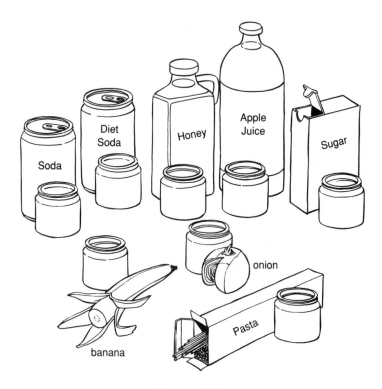

Figure 10.1

4. Add 1 tablespoon (15 ml) of distilled water to each jar containing a solid food sample.

5. Prepare a data table such as the one shown here. *Note:* List all eight food samples.

Data Table			
Results			
Food Sample	Initial Color	Final Color	Sugar Concentration
soda			
diet soda			
honey			
apple juice			

6. Test for the presence of monosaccharides in each food sample by:
- adding 1 tablespoon (15 ml) of testing solution to the jar.
- observing and recording the color of the solution in the jar.
- setting the jar in a pot of boiling water and heating for three minutes.
- using forceps or a pot holder to carefully remove the hot jar.
- observe and record the color of the solution in the jar again.

7. Determine the concentration of the monosaccharide present in each food sample by comparing the final color of the solution with the following color chart:

blue—zero

green—low concentration

light to dark yellow—moderate concentration

orange to red—high concentration

Results

The author's results indicated that the soda, honey, apple juice, and onion had the highest amount of simple sugars; the banana, a moderate amount; and the pasta, diet soda and table sugar (sucrose), no monosaccharides. *Note:* The results will vary depending on the brand of food tested and on the conditions and length of time the food has been stored.

Why?

The monosaccharide testing reagent contains copper II ions (Cu^{++}). Solutions containing copper II ions are blue. Sugars such as glucose and fructose provide electrons needed to change the copper II ions to copper I ions (Cu^+) and elemental copper (Cu^0). These simple sugars function as reducing agents because they provide electrons during a chemical reaction. The color of the copper testing solution changes from blue to red as the copper II ions are first changed into copper I and then elemental copper. With disaccharides or polysaccharides, the testing solution remains blue.

Try New Approaches

1. Test other food products by repeating the experiment. **Science Fair Hint:** Prepare a bar graph to compare the monosaccharide content of each food sample tested.

2. Fruits and vegetables change chemically as they continue to ripen. Taken straight from the garden, they may test negative for the presence of simple sugars. Once they are picked, their carbohydrates (in the form of starches and disaccharides) begin to break down into simple sugars. Demonstrate this change by repeating the experiment using fresh fruits and/or vegetables. A cluster of grapes provides a sample that can be tested daily to observe any changes in the monosaccharide level of the ripening fruit.

3. Milk contains lactose, which is a **polysaccharide** (large molecules containing many simple sugars bonded together). Does heat break this polysaccharide into monosaccharides? Repeat the original experiment using milk as the food source. Observe the color after three minutes of heating; then continue to heat the milk for five additional minutes and observe again.

Design Your Own Experiment

1. Starch and cellulose are polysaccharides. Use drops of tincture of iodine to distinguish between starch and cellulose. **CAUTION:** Keep the iodine out of reach of small children. It is poisonous and is for external use only. Starch turns blue-violet to black when iodine touches it, but cellulose does not alter the reddish brown color of iodine. Demonstrate this by putting several drops of iodine on a slice of apple and on a slice of white potato (see Figure 10.2).

2a. During the human digestive process, macromolecules of starch are chemically changed into glucose. Much of this change occurs in your mouth. Demonstrate this by cutting two small, equal-size pieces from a slice of bread. Place one piece in your mouth and chew it 30 times. It will become very mushy. Make an effort to mix as much saliva as possible with the bread. Spit the mushy bread and saliva mixture onto a piece of wax paper. Place the dry piece of bread on a separate piece of wax paper. Test for the presence of starch by adding four drops of iodine to each sample.

b. Test for the presence of monosaccharides in the bread before and after it is chewed. Repeat the experiment two times, first using a dry piece of bread, and then chewing the bread 30 times and testing the mushy bread and saliva mixture.

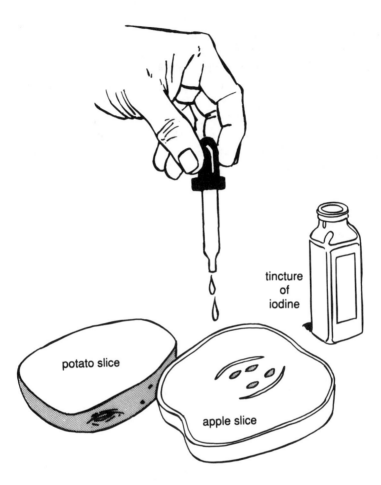

Figure 10.2

Get the Facts

1. Sucrose is a double sugar called a *disaccharide*. It is represented by the formula $C_{12}H_{22}O_{11}$. Glucose is known as *blood sugar* because it is the sugar transported by the blood to cells where it is used as a fuel to make energy. Fructose is found in fruits and honey and is much sweeter than sucrose or glucose. Glucose and fructose are simple sugars, and both are represented by the formula $C_6H_{12}O_6$, but the arrangement of the atoms within these sugars is different. Find out more about the physical structure of these sugars and how it affects their chemical behavior. Which sugar is an aldo-hexose? Which is a keto-hexose? What products are produced by the hydrolysis of sucrose, maltose, and lactose (examples of complex sugars)?

2. Starch serves as a nutrient and is found in plant products such as grains, fruits, and vegetables. Cellulose, like starch, is a carbohydrate. Although it is not easily digested by humans, it is important as the dietary fiber commonly called *roughage*. Use a chemistry text to find out more about the physical properties of these two chemicals. What is the difference between their molecular structures? How do the tastes of starch, cellulose, and sugars compare?

Indicators: Identifying Acids and Bases

11

Certain compounds react in acidic and/or basic solutions to form substances with specific colors. These compounds, or "indicators," can be used to identify the acidic or basic properties of household materials and foods.

In this project, you will determine the effect of acids and bases on homemade indicators. Carbon dioxide in exhaled breath will be tested for acidic properties, and you will determine whether exercise increases the carbon dioxide content in exhaled breath. You will also examine the pH (relative acidity) of a solution, and the effect of pH on indicators.

Getting Started

Purpose: To determine the effect that acids and bases have on the color of red cabbage extract.

Materials

1-quart (1-liter) clear glass jar	masking tape
red cabbage extract (see Appendix 5)	4 baby-food jars
distilled water	white vinegar
marking pen	2 eyedroppers

Procedure

CAUTION: Handle the ammonia with care and work in a well-ventilated area. Ammonia is poisonous, and its fumes can damage skin and the mucous membranes of the nose, mouth, and eyes.

1. Fill the quart (liter) jar half full with the red cabbage extract.

2. Add distilled water to fill the jar so that the liquid is clear enough to see through but retains a definite purple color.

3. With the marking pen, write "Cabbage Indicator" on a piece of masking tape and tape this label to the jar.

4. Fill two baby-food jars one-fourth full with the diluted cabbage extract.

5. Fill a third baby-food jar one-fourth full with vinegar, label it "Acid," and place one eyedropper in this jar.

6. Fill a fourth baby-food jar one-fourth full with ammonia, label it "Base," and place the other eyedropper in this jar.

7. Add drops of the acidic solution to one small jar of the cabbage indicator; swirl the jar to mix the solution after each addition. Continue until a definite color change is observed.

8. Add drops of the basic solution to the other small jar of cabbage indicator; swirl to mix. Continue until a definite color change is observed (see Figure 11.1).

Results

The ammonia, a base, changes the cabbage extract to green. The vinegar, an acid, changes the cabbage extract to a pinkish red.

Why?

An **indicator** is a compound that changes color in the presence of an acid or a base. The color of any material is due to the chemical makeup of the substance that affects the light waves absorbed and reflected. **Bases,** solutions containing **hydroxide ions** (OH^-), change the chemical structure of the cabbage so that it reflects more green light waves. **Acids,** solutions containing **hydrogen ions** (H^+) change the structure of the cabbage so that it reflects more red light waves. These specific color changes allow red cabbage to be used to indicate the presence of an acid or a base.

Try New Approaches

1. Use the instructions in Appendix 5 for preparing red cabbage extract to prepare extracts from other substances, such as blueberries, beets, grapes, or cherries. Repeat the experiment to determine the color changes of these extracts in the presence of an acid or a base. Not all indicators are affected by both acids and bases. You may discover an indicator that is specific (only changes color for an acid or a base).

Figure 11.1

2. Turmeric is an indicator specific for the testing of a base. Prepare this indicator by adding ½ teaspoon (2.5 ml) of turmeric powder to ½ cup (125 ml) of rubbing alcohol. Repeat the original experiment to determine the color change in the presence of a base and the effect, if any, of an acid on the indicator.

Design Your Own Experiment

1. Use the food extracts previously prepared (red cabbage, blueberries, beets, grapes, or cherries) to test the acidic or basic properties of household materials, such as liquid and powder cleansers, cream of tartar, fruit juices, baking powder, and baking soda. Make solutions of the dry materials by adding 1 teaspoon (5 ml) of powder to ¼ cup (63 ml) of distilled water. For each test, fill a small baby food jar one-fourth full with the food extract and add 1 teaspoon (5 ml) of testing solution. Record the color and determine whether the solution has acidic or basic properties. Prepare a data table such as the one shown on the next page.

2. Indicator testing paper can be made by soaking coffee filters in different liquid indicators made from food extracts, such as the red cabbage extract or the turmeric and alcohol solution. Allow the papers

Data Table					
Food Extracts					
Material Tested	Red Cabbage	Blueberries	Beets	Grapes	Cherries
powder cleanser					
baking powder					
lemon juice					

to dry, then cut them into 1-×-¼-inch (2.5-×-6.3-cm) strips and store them in a closed container. Test for acids and bases by dipping about ¼ inch (0.63 cm) of each testing paper into the solution. Observe the resulting color of each paper. Allow the paper strips to dry and display them on a poster board (see Figure 11.2).

3. Demonstrate that paper indicators can be used to test for the acidic or basic nature of gases, such as ammonia, that are very soluble in water. Wet a piece of turmeric paper with water. Hold the wet paper above, but not touching, the mouth of an open bottle of household ammonia. Prepare and display drawings of the results. The ammonia gas dissolves in the water, and the product of this combination causes the turmeric to change colors. Write a chemical equation showing the combination of ammonia and water. Identify the product as an acid or a base and use the results of the turmeric paper to confirm this identification.

4a. Carbon dioxide gas in your exhaled breath chemically reacts with water to produce an acid. Test for the presence of this acid by exhaling through a drinking straw into a glass soda bottle half filled with a solution of brom thymol blue indicator. (See Appendix 5) Hold a bottle of brom thymol blue indicator nearby to make the color comparison easier to see. A white background and good lighting will also make the comparison easier.

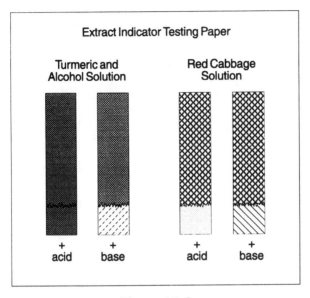

Extract Indicator Testing Paper

Turmeric and Alcohol Solution   Red Cabbage Solution

+ acid   + base   + acid   + base

Figure 11.2

b. Determine if exercise increases the concentration of carbon dioxide in exhaled breath by repeating the previous experiment after exercising. An increase in the rate of change and in the intensity of the color indicates an increase in carbon dioxide. Use photographs to represent the procedure and display an equation for the reaction along with them.

5. Soil can have acidic or basic characteristics. Test the acidic/basic nature of a soil sample by combining 1 cup (250 ml) of soil with 2 cups (500 ml) of hot tap water. Stir well. Pour the mixture into a large funnel lined with filter paper. Fill a baby food jar half full with the **filtrate** (liquid that has passed through the filter paper). Fill the jar with red cabbage extract and stir. Use the color of the filtrate to determine its acidic or basic nature.

Get the Facts

1. Each indicator has a particular concentration range over which the color change occurs. The measurement of the concentration of an acidic or a basic solution can be expressed as its *pH;* thus, indicators are affected by solutions with a specific pH. Find out more about indicators and the pH that affects them. What is the pH a measure of? Make a list of different indicators and their pH range.

2. The pigment in red cabbage belongs to a class of compounds known as *anthocyanins*. The red color of apples is also due to an anthocyanin pigment. Find out more about the anthocyanin pigment. How is its color affected by the presence of an acid? A base? One source of information is "Solar Photography" in Janice VanCleave's *A+ Projects in Biology* (New York: Wiley, 1993).

12 Acids and Bases: Their Neutralization

Water solutions of any acid taste sour and react with certain metals to liberate hydrogen gas. Bases in water have a bitter taste and feel slippery.

In this project, you will examine the differences between acids and bases and the neutralizing effect of adding the two chemicals. The titration process will be used to determine the amount of acetylsalicylic acid in various brands of aspirin tablets as well as the strength of different antacid tablets. You will also look at the pH–pOH scale and explore methods of determining the pH and pOH.

Getting Started

Purpose: To determine how an acid is neutralized.

Materials

3 baby-food jars

sheet of white paper

3 eyedroppers

white vinegar

phenolphthalein (see Appendix 5)

household ammonia

spoon

Procedure

CAUTION: Handle the ammonia with care and work in a well-ventilated area. Ammonia is poisonous, and its fumes can damage skin and the mucous membranes of the nose, mouth, and eyes.

1. To prepare for the experiment, set the baby-food jars on a sheet of white paper so that you can detect color changes easily. Set aside a separate eyedropper for the vinegar, phenolphthalein, and ammonia.

2. Add 25 drops of vinegar (an acid) to one jar.

3. Add three or four drops of phenolphthalein and stir to test for the effect of this liquid on an acid.

4. Record any color changes.

5. Add 25 drops of ammonia (a base) to the second jar.

6. Add three or four drops of phenolphthalein and stir to test for the effect of this liquid on a base.

7. Record any color changes.

8. Add 25 drops of vinegar to the third jar.

9. Add three or four drops of phenolphthalein and then neutralize this acid with a base by adding a few drops of ammonia.

10. Continue to add drops of ammonia until the entire solution retains a pale pink color after stirring (see Figure 12.1).

Results

There is no change in color when phenolphthalein is added to the vinegar, but the solution turns pink when phenolphthalein is added to the ammonia. At first, adding ammonia causes no color change in the vinegar. Eventually, the area around the ammonia drop turns pink, but the color disappears when the solution is mixed. A quantity of ammonia is finally added that results in a pale pink color that does not disappear.

Why?

Vinegar is an acid, and like all acids, it contains hydrogen ions (H^+). Household ammonia is a basic solution and is identified as a base by the presence of hydroxide ions (OH^-). Indicators are chemicals that change colors in the presence of hydrogen and/or hydroxide ions. They change because the chemical structure of a material determines how it absorbs and reflects light waves, and therefore its color. Phenolphthalein is an indicator that specifically determines the presence of a base because when combined with hydroxide ions, its chemical structure changes and reflects pink light, giving a pink color.

In a neutralization reaction, an acid and a base react to form a salt and water. In this experiment, vinegar and household ammonia combine to form the salt ammonium acetate, and the H^+ and OH^- ions combine to form water (HOH) molecules. That is,

$$HC_2H_3O_2 \quad + \quad NH_4OH \quad \longrightarrow \quad NH_4C_2H_3O_2 \quad + \quad HOH$$

vinegar plus *household ammonia* yields *ammonium acetate* plus *water*

When all of the hydrogen ions from the acid combine with all of the hydroxide ions from the base, the solution is considered **neutral.** The solution is neither acidic nor basic and thus does not affect the indicator. In

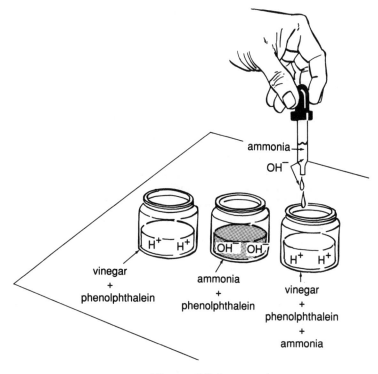

Figure 12.1

this experiment, the hydroxide ions in each drop of ammonia combine with the hydrogen ions in the vinegar until all of the hydrogen ions are neutralized. The resulting pink color of the solution indicates that all of the acid is neutralized and that a few extra hydroxide ions are present to react with the phenolphthalein indicator.

Try New Approaches

1. Would neutralizing the ammonia solution with vinegar make a difference in the results that are observed? Start with step 8 of the procedure and repeat the experiment replacing the vinegar in the jar with the ammonia and adding the vinegar until the color disappears. Study the chemical equation for the reaction between vinegar (acetic acid) and ammonia (ammonium hydroxide) to determine whether adding one chemical to the other affects the product of the reaction.

2. Can other indicators be used as effectively as phenolphthalein?

   a. See the experiment in Chapter 11 for information about indicators you can make and use. Repeat the original experiment using different homemade indicators.

   b. A commercially prepared indicator such as methyl orange can be purchased with the assistance of your science teacher. This indicator is red in acidic solutions and yellow in basic solutions.

3. Adding a measured volume of base to a measured volume of acid is done in a laboratory procedure known as **titration.** Titration is used to determine the **normality** (number of equivalents of solute per liter of solution) concentration of an acidic or a basic solution. In such a procedure, an acid with a known concentration is added to a base of unknown concentration, or a base with a known concentration is added to an acid of unknown concentration. An indicator is used to determine when the solution is neutral. Repeat the original experiment using the eyedropper to titrate the vinegar with the household ammonia. Carefully count the number of drops of household ammonia needed to neutralize the 25 drops of vinegar. The normality (N) of acetic acid is about 0.83 N in the 5% vinegar solution used. Use the normality concentration of the acetic acid, the data from the experiment, and the following equation to determine the normality concentration of the household ammonia. See Appendix 7 for an example calculation.

$$N \text{ (acid)} \times V \text{ (acid)} = N \text{ (base)} \times V \text{ (base)}$$

Note: In this equation, N = normality and V = volume.

Design Your Own Experiment

1. The acetylsalicylic acid in aspirin reduces sensitivity to minor aches and pains. Do expensive brands of aspirin tablets give you more for your money? Determine the amount of acid in different-priced aspirin tablets by dissolving each tablet tested in 50 ml of distilled water. Add three to four drops of phenolphthalein. Titrate with household ammonia by adding drops of ammonia until the solution retains a pale pink color. Record information needed to determine the normality concentration of each aspirin solution in a data table such as the one shown on the next page.

Data Table				
	Acid		Base	
Aspirin Brand	Normality	Volume	Normality	Volume

2. Compare the strength of different brands of antacid tablets by dissolving each tablet tested in ¼ cup (63 ml) of distilled water. Add three to four drops of phenolphthalein. Titrate with 5% (0.83 N) white vinegar by adding the vinegar one drop at a time with an eyedropper until the pink color disappears. See Appendix 8 for instructions on determining the volume of each drop of liquid from an eyedropper. Use the volume of the acid needed to neutralize the base to determine the normality concentration of each antacid solution. Design a data table to record your experimental data.

Get the Facts

1. Acidic and basic characteristics are expressed by numbers known as the *pH* and *pOH*. Find out what the pH and pOH measure. What equations are used to calculate the pH and pOH values?

2. A measuring system known as the *pH–pOH scale* is used to indicate the concentration of an acid or a base. The letter *p* is from the Danish word *potenz*, which means "strength"; pH is the strength of the hydrogen ions; pOH is the strength of the hydroxide ions. Water is said to be neutral and thus has an equal number of H^+ and OH^- ions. Water and other neutral solutions have a pH of 7. Find out more about this measuring system. What is the range of the scale? What does an increase in the pH number indicate? Make a chart representing common substances at various pH and pOH values.

3. There is more than one definition of acid and base. The one given in this project (an acid is any chemical that produces hydrogen ions in a

solution, and a base is any chemical that produces hydroxide ions in a solution) was proposed by Svante Arrhenius, a Swedish chemist. Use a chemistry text to find other definitions of acids and bases, such as the Bronsted and Lowry definition and the Gilbert Newton Lewis definition.

13 | Phase Changes: Effects of Solutes

Phase changes, such as melting, freezing, evaporation, and condensation, occur whenever the physical phase (gas, liquid, or solid) of a substance changes. Solutes may play a significant role in these changes. Salt, for example, is used to melt ice on sidewalks and to make ice colder in an ice-cream maker.

In this project, you will determine the freezing and boiling points of water and the effect of salt and other solutes on these temperatures. Colligative properties, which depend only on the number of particles in a solution, will be studied and used to calculate the freezing-point depression and boiling-point elevation of solutions.

Getting Started

Purpose: To determine the boiling point of water and plot a time–temperature graph of the phase change.

Materials

1 quart (1 liter) of distilled
water

2-quart (2-liter) cooking pot

fondue fork (or heavy wire)

candy thermometer

stove

Procedure

1. Pour the distilled water into the pot.
2. Place the fondue fork (or heavy wire) across the pot and clip the thermometer to the fork so that the bulb is suspended in the middle of the water (see Figure 13.1)
3. Read and record the temperature of the water in a data table such as the one shown on the next page.
4. Place the pot of water on the stove.
5. Heat at a medium temperature.
6. Every 15 seconds, read and record the temperature until the water stops getting hotter and three readings of the same temperature are recorded. *Note:* This should take about six minutes.

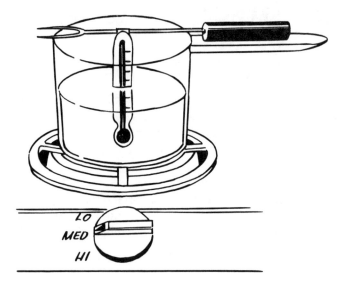

Figure 13.1

Data Table		
Time (seconds)	Temperature (°F or °C)	Observation
0		
15		

7. Observe and make note of the appearance of the water each time the temperature is recorded.

8. Plot the results on a graph with the temperature on the vertical axis and the time on the horizontal axis (see Figure 13.2).

Results

As the temperature increases, tiny bubbles appear on the bottom and around the sides of the pot. The bubbles increase in size and begin to break at the surface of the water as the water temperature reaches (exactly or approximately) 212°F (100°C). The bubbles continue to break at the surface, but the temperature remains constant.

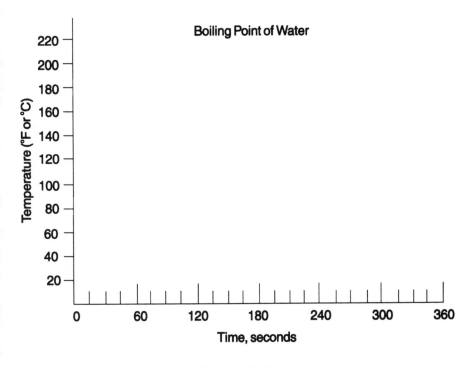

Figure 13.2

Why?

Certain conditions are required to effect a **phase change** of matter from one **physical phase** (gas, liquid, or solid) to another. Heating the water in the pot causes vapor bubbles to form on the bottom and around the sides of the pot where the water is the hottest. As the bubbles rise through the cooler water, they not only cool but also are pressed from all sides by the water molecules, causing them to collapse (see Figure 13.3).

As the water temperature increases, the pressure inside the vapor bubbles increases. Eventually, the **boiling point** is reached (a temperature at which the pressure inside the bubbles equals the atmospheric pressure outside). At the boiling point, the bubbles do not collapse but escape from the surface of the water.

During boiling, the temperature of the vapor is the same as that of the liquid. The **kinetic energy** (energy of motion) of liquids is less than that of vapor. Because of the lesser amount of kinetic energy, liquid molecules move less and are more closely bonded together. It takes extra energy to physically break the bonding between liquid molecules and change them into gas. At the boiling point of a liquid, the energy applied by the heating source does not increase the water's temperature but is used in the phase change from liquid to gas.

Try New Approaches

1. Does increasing the heat source raise the temperature of the water? Repeat the experiment using a higher heat setting on the stove.

2a. Does adding a **solute** (substance dissolved in a solution) to the water affect the boiling-point temperature of the water? Repeat the original experiment adding ½ cup (125 ml) of sodium chloride (table salt) to the water.

b. Does using a different solute change the results? Repeat the original experiment adding ½ cup (125 ml) of sucrose (table sugar) to the water. **Science Fair Hint:** Use neatly labeled graphs as part of a display.

Design Your Own Experiment

1a. At what temperature does the **freezing** (the physical change from a liquid to a solid) of water occur? The temperature of a mixture of ice and water will change until the freezing point (or the melting

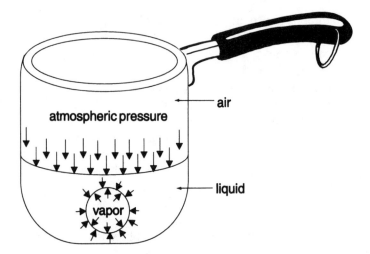

Figure 13.3

point) is reached. At the freezing point, the temperature of the solution remains constant as energy is used in the phase change. Demonstrate this by filling an ice-cube tray with distilled water and placing it in a freezer overnight. Fill a drinking glass half full with these pure ice cubes (made with distilled water) and cover the ice with distilled water. Insert a thermometer into the glass of ice water. Set the glass in a large can. Fill the can with ice (this does not have to be pure ice) mixed with 1 cup (250 ml) of table salt. Gently stir with the thermometer. Read and record the temperature every 15 seconds. Add pure ice as the cubes in the glass melt. Continue stirring and recording the temperature until a constant temperature is reached.

b. Does adding a solute to the water affect the temperature of the ice water? Repeat this experiment adding 4 tablespoons (60 ml) of table salt to the ice water in the glass.

c. Rock salt is added to ice in an ice-cream maker to lower the temperature. Is rock salt more effective at lowering the temperature than table salt is? Repeat this experiment using rock salt instead of table salt. Use information about **colligative properties** (properties that depend only on the number of particles in solution) to explain the results.

2. Do solutes affect the freezing of water? Fill two 5-ounce (150-ml) cups with distilled water. Dissolve 1 tablespoon (15 ml) of salt in one of the cups of water. Label the cup containing the salt with the letter *S*. Set both cups in a freezer. Check the cups every hour for one day; then leave the cups in the freezer overnight.

3. Place the frayed end of a 12-inch (30-cm) cotton string on top of an ice cube. Rub the ice as you press the string against it. The string should cover as much of the surface of the ice as it can and lay flat against the ice. Sprinkle 1 teaspoon (5 ml) of salt over the string. Wait for one minute and gently lift the string. The ice cube should be stuck to the string and it should be possible to suspend the cube by holding the string up. A brief explanation is that rubbing the ice as you press the string onto it melts the ice and that water is absorbed by the string. The salt also melts the ice. The salt then dissolves in the water, producing a salty solution that freezes at a lower temperature than the freezing temperature of water, which is 32°F (0°C). The temperature of the salty water surrounding the string is lower than the freezing temperature of any unsalted water absorbed by the string; thus, the pure water in the string freezes and sticks to the ice cube. Improve upon this explanation and include information about freezing-point depression and the fact that some of the lower-concentration salty water freezes.

Get the Facts

1. A solution has a different boiling point and freezing point than a pure solvent because of the colligative properties of the solution. Colligative properties depend only on the number of particles dissolved in the solvent and not on the nature of the solute or solvent. Find out more about the effects of colligative properties on solutions, including vapor-pressure lowering, boiling-point elevation, and freezing-point depression. How much of a pressure and temperature change can solutes make? Why does salty ice water have a lower temperature than ice water without the salt? Why are icy sidewalks sprinkled with salt or sand?

2. The freezing and boiling points of a solution can be predetermined with the *molal* freezing-point and boiling-point constants for the solvent. Use a chemistry text to find out about these constants for water. Use the boiling-point constant to calculate the accepted boiling point of solutions containing sugar and salt. Compare the accepted values with your experimental values.

14 Colloids: Dispersed Particles

The environment abounds with colloidal materials. In these suspensions, small particles are permanently dispersed throughout the solvent.

In this project, you will identify the dimensions of colloidal substances and distinguish between pure solutions and colloidal systems. You will also look at the effect of temperature and pH on the coagulation of colloidal particles and determine their adsorbing properties.

Getting Started

Purpose: To use light to distinguish a colloidal suspension from a pure solution.

Materials

cardboard box about 1 foot (30 cm) square

scissors

ruler

pencil

3 1-quart (1-liter) glass jars at least 6 inches (15 cm) tall

distilled water

marking pen

masking tape

½ teaspoon (2.5 ml) of table salt (sodium chloride)

eyedropper

whole milk

flashlight

Procedure

1. Turn the cardboard box upside down.
2. Cut a viewing hole 4 inches (10 cm) square in the front of the box. *Note:* The hole should be 2 inches (5 cm) from the left front corner and 2 inches (5 cm) from the bottom of the box (see A in Figure 14.1).
3. Use the point of the pencil to make a small hole in the left side of the box. *Note:* The hole should be 4 inches (10 cm) from the front corner and 4 inches (10 cm) from the bottom of the box (see B in Figure 14.1).

4. Fill the jars with distilled water.
5. With the marking pen, write "Water" on a piece of masking tape and tape this label to one jar.
6. Stir the salt into the second jar. Label this jar "Solution."
7. With the eyedropper, add one drop of milk to the third jar of water and stir. Label this jar "Colloid."
8. Place the jar labeled "Water" under the box. *Note:* The jar should be centered in front of both the viewing hole and the small hole in the side of the box (see C in Figure 14.1).
9. Hold the flashlight near the small hole in the side of the box.
10. Look through the viewing hole and observe the effect that the liquid has on the light rays.
11. Repeat the procedure using the jars labeled "Solution" and "Colloid."

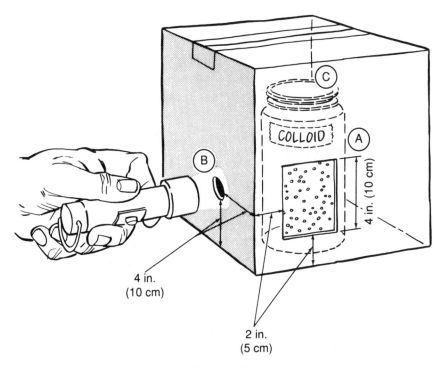

Figure 14.1

Results

The light passes through the liquids in the jars labeled "Water" and "Solution." The milky water, however, has a pale bluish gray appearance.

Why?

The rays pass unchanged through the "water" because there are no particles to scatter the light through the solution and because the sodium and chloride ions, with diameters of 7.87×10^{-9} inch (0.00000002 cm) and 1.42×10^{-8} inch (0.000000036 cm) respectively, are too small to affect the light noticeably.

The particles in milk cluster into micelles. **Colloidal micelles** are submicroscopic clumps of material ranging in diameter from 3.94×10^{-8} inch (0.0000001 cm) to 3.94×10^{-5} inch (0.0001 cm). These globules are dispersed throughout the milky water, and they separate the small, blue light waves in the beam of light. The scattered blue rays give the milky solution a bluish gray appearance.

The fact that colloidal particles scatter light to all sides was first discovered by John Tyndall, a British physicist. By shining a light beam through liquids, we can use this **Tyndall effect** to distinguish between a pure solution and a colloidal dispersion.

Try New Approaches

Use the Tyndall effect to distinguish between pure solutions and colloidal dispersions in different samples. For each sample, mix together ½ teaspoon (2.5 ml) of solute with 1 quart (1 liter) of water. *Note:* First perform the original experiment to determine whether the water you are using scatters light. If it does not, it can be used instead of distilled water. Examples of solutes to be added to the water are sucrose (table sugar), prepared mustard, soap (try different types), syrup, ketchup, and gelatin (heat the water to dissolve the gelatin).

Design Your Own Experiment

1. Can micelles in a liquid colloidal mixture be separated from the liquid by filtration? Homogenized milk is an example of a colloidal dispersion of solids (fats, proteins, and lactose) in a liquid (water). Stand a funnel in a drinking glass. Fold a paper towel in half twice. Fit the closed point inside the funnel and pull one layer of the paper against the top of the funnel (see Figure 14.2). Pour about 1 cup (250 ml) of

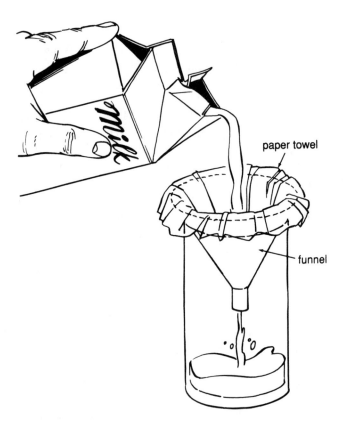

Figure 14.2

milk into the paper-lined funnel. After the filtrate has drained through the paper, examine the paper for evidence of any **residue** (solid separated from the mixture). Try other colloidal mixtures.

2. Colloidal particles can be made to **coagulate** (come together or clump).

   a. Changing the temperature of a material can cause coagulation. Demonstrate this by preparing gelatin by following the instructions on the packet. The hot liquid gelatin is called a **sol**. When cooled, the sol becomes a solid gel. Allow the gel to sit at room temperature and observe its change back to a liquid sol.

   b. Changing the pH of a material can cause coagulation. Demonstrate this by adding 1 tablespoon (15 ml) of vinegar (acetic acid) to 1 cup (250 ml) of milk. Even though colloidal systems are electrically neutral, the positive and negative charges are not always equally dispersed. The suspended micelles can have an excess of one charge, while the dispersing medium has an excess of another. When the number of positive and negative charges on the particles is equal, the positive and negative particles are attracted to one another, and the colloid collagulates.

3a. The unique properties of colloids are primarily attributed to the extremely large surface area presented by the colloidal particles, compared to the minute surface area of dissolved particles in solutions. Atoms or molecules on the surface of particles of colloidal size tend to attract substances with which they come into contact. This surface attraction is known as **adsorption.**

Demonstrate adsorbent properties of particles by mixing together in a 1-quart (1-liter) jar, ten drops of green food coloring, 1 cup (250 ml) of water, and 1 tablespoon (15 ml) of activated carbon. (Activated carbon is used in fish aquarium filters; it is sold in pet stores.) Make a control by preparing a second jar, omitting the activated carbon. Secure the lids on both jars and gently shake the jars a few times. Shake the jars two or three times each day for five days. Compare the color of the water in each jar each day.

b. Dividing a substance into particles of colloidal size greatly increases its surface area. Homogenized milk has colloidal-size fat globules evenly spread throughout the liquid. The total outside surface area of each separate drop of fat is greater than the surface area would be if the large drop of fat formed by combining all the little drops.

Demonstrate this fact by stacking 27 separate cubes (blocks or sugar cubes) together to form one large cube. First, determine the total surface area of the large cube by using the following formula:

surface area = length × width × 6 sides

Second, calculate the total surface area of each of the 27 separate cubes by finding the area of one cube and multiplying its surface area by 27. For example, in Figure 14.3, the surface area of the large cube would be 864 square inches (5,400 cm²) as compared to 2,592 square inches (16,200 cm²) for the 27 separate cubes making up the large cube. The calculations for the surface area of the large cube and the 27 small cubes are as follows:

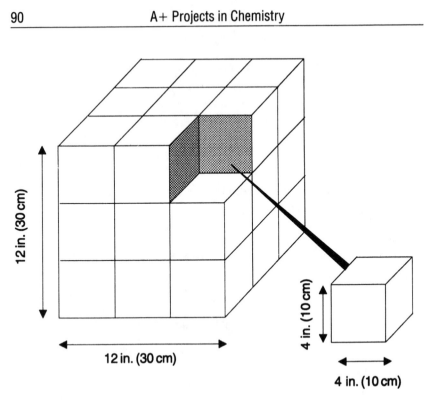

Figure 14.3

surface area = 12 inches × 12 inches (30 cm × 30 cm) ×
(large cube)   6 sides
            = 864 square inches (5,400 cm^2)

surface area = 4 inches × 4 inches (10 cm × 10 cm) ×
(27 cubes)   6 sides × 27 cubes
            = 2,592 square inches (16,200 cm^2)

Get the Facts

Can colloids form when any one of the three phases of matter—solid, liquid, and gas—disperses in one of the others? Find out more about the kinds of colloidal dispersions. Provide examples of each type of colloidal dispersion, such as a solid dispersed in a liquid (for example, toothpaste). Use a biology text to include in your findings information about colloidal systems in the cells of animals.

15 Electrolytes: Conductors of Electricity

Electricity is fundamental to nature. It is utilized in the form of electric currents. Electrolytes are chemicals that conduct an electric current in a water solution. Not all solutions conduct electricity.

In this project, you will identify common electrolytes and compare their strengths. The electrolysis of water and brine will be studied. You will also look at the history of electrolytic cells and construct a simple electrolytic cell.

Getting Started

Purpose: To determine whether table salt is an electrolyte.

Materials

duct tape	spoon
3 "D" cell batteries	ruler
2 teaspoons (10 ml) of table salt (sodium chloride)	scissors
	aluminum foil
½ cup (125 ml) of distilled water	flashlight bulb
cereal bowl	

Procedure

CAUTION: Do not use batteries other than "D" cell batteries and do not use more than three "D" cell batteries. Electricity can be dangerous.

1. Tape the three batteries together with the positive end of one touching the negative end of the other.

2. Combine the salt and water in the bowl. Stir well.

3. Measure and cut a strip of aluminum foil 4 inches (10 cm) wide × 12 inches (30 cm) long.

4. Fold the foil strip lengthwise four times so that the strip is ¼ inch (0.64 cm) wide and 12 inches (30 cm) long.

5. Stand the flat, negative end of the connected batteries in the bowl of salty water.

6. Wrap one end of the foil strip around the metal base of the flashlight bulb.

7. Hold the foil strip tightly around the base and press it against the raised, positive end of the connected batteries.

8. Lay the free end of the foil strip under the surface of the salty water in the bowl so that it is near, but not touching, the connected batteries (see Figure 15.1).

Result

The bulb glows.

Why?

An **electric current** is produced by a flow of electric charges. In metals, the current is due to a flow of electrons and is called **metallic conduction.** In a solution, the current is due to movement of **ions** (positive and negative particles) and is called **ionic conduction.** In this experiment, the electric current is carried by electrons in the aluminum foil and in metals in the battery as well as by ions in the salt solution. The bulb glows because as the electric current passes through the filament of the bulb, the filament heats up and gives off light.

The electrons do not flow spontaneously. They must be caused to flow by an electric force from the battery. The negative end of the battery repels electrons, and the positive end of the battery draws electrons toward it. Electrons do not flow out the **cathode** (negative terminal) of the battery and swim through the solution to the aluminum foil strip attached to the **anode** (positive terminal). Instead, at the negative terminal, cations (positive particles) in the solution accept electrons; at the positive terminal, **anions** (negative particles) give up electrons. The space between the foil strip and the battery is "bridged" as the ions in solution remove electrons from one side and add electrons to the opposite side of the gap.

Try New Approaches

1. Sodium chloride (table salt) is an **electrolyte** (a compound that conducts an electric current in a water solution or in a molten state). Test

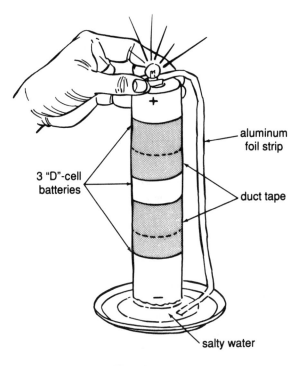

aluminum
foil strip

3 "D"-cell
batteries

duct tape

salty water

Figure 15.1

other substances to determine whether they are electrolytes or non-electrolytes. Repeat the experiment replacing the salt with materials such as table sugar (sucrose) and Epsom salts (magnesium sulfate).

2. The number of ions in a solution is directly proportional to the conductivity of the solution; that is, the greater the number of ions, the greater the intensity of the bulb's glow. Repeat the original experiment replacing the salt with solid materials (sugar and Epsom salts) and then using solutions such as vinegar, soda, fruit juices, milk, and other liquid foods. Remove the negative end of the connected batteries and the foil from the bowl and wash with distilled water after each test. Compare the electrolytic strength of each solution by comparing how intensely the bulb glows. **Science Fair Hint:** Display the testing materials with drawings indicating the intensity of the light produced by each testing material.

3. Does the number of batteries change the intensity of the light? The energy for pushing the electric current through the filament in the bulb comes from chemical reactions in the batteries. Use a chemistry text to find out how batteries (electrochemical cells) release electrical energy. Test the effect of connecting batteries by repeating the original experiment two times, first using one battery, and then using two batteries. (Remember, do not use more than three batteries.)

Design Your Own Experiment

1a. **Electrolysis** is the process by which an electric current is used to cause a chemical change. Distilled water does not conduct an electric current, because no ions are present. The presence of a small amount of an electrolyte, such as sodium chloride, allows the solution to conduct and the electrolysis of water to take place. The products of the electrolysis of water are hydrogen and oxygen.

Demonstrate the electrolysis of water by filling a drinking glass with distilled water to within 1 inch (2.54 cm) from the top. Add ¼ teaspoon (1.25 ml) of table salt to the water and stir. Cut a stiff piece of paper to cover the top of the glass. Straighten the ends of two paper clips, leaving a hook on one end of each. Insert the paper clips through the stiff paper so that they are about 1 inch (2.5 cm) apart. Place the paper over the top of the glass of salty water. Prepare two aluminum foil strips as in the original experiment. Wrap one end of each strip around the hooked end of each paper clip. With your fingers, hold the free ends of the strips against the ends of a "D" cell battery. Observe the ends of the paper clips extending beneath the surface of the water (see Figure 15.2). Read about the electrolysis of water in a chemistry text to determine the chemical reactions occurring at each paper clip terminal. Use a drawing with equations indicating the changes at the cathode and anode.

b. Chlorine, hydrogen, and sodium hydroxide are important industrial chemicals produced by the electrolysis of **brine** (a concentrated solution of sodium chloride). Find out more about this process and display a diagram showing the electrolyte in solution as well as the reaction at the anode and cathode. Indicate methods of separating the three chemicals.

2. A simple battery that produces a safe amount of electric current can be made from a lemon, a steel paper clip, and a brass thumbtack. Cut the lemon in half. Stick the thumbtack and the paper clip into the pulp of one of the lemon halves. The tack and clip should be as close

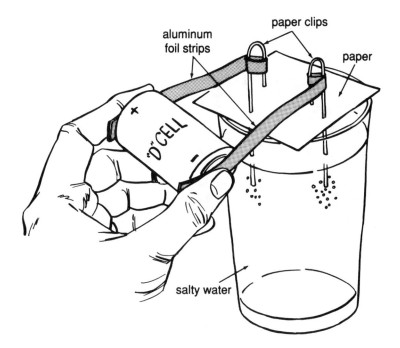

Figure 15.2

as possible to each other without touching. Take care not to get any lemon juice on the tops of the tack and the clip. Moisten your tongue with saliva and barely touch the tip of your tongue to the tops of the tack and the clip (see Figure 15.3). The taste sensation is due to the small amount of electric current resulting from the electrolytes in the saliva on your tongue.

Get the Facts

1. Luigi Galvani, a medical professor, and Alessandro Volta, a physicist, were the first to experiment with producing electrical energy from chemicals. Find out more about the experiments performed by Galvani that caused him to believe that within animals existed "animal electricity." What experiments made Volta violently oppose Galvani's animal electricity theory?

2. The *deposition* (depositing) of a thin layer of a metal on an object in an electrolytic cell is called *electroplating*. Find out more about this pro-

tongue

brass thumb tack

steel paper clip

Figure 15.3

cess. What is electroforming? Electrowinning? Electrorefining? Electropolishing? Electromachining?

3. Until the end of the nineteenth century, only the very wealthy could afford aluminum items. They were expensive because there was no known practical way of separating the pure metal from aluminum compounds. The inexpensive aluminum used today is produced by an adaptation of an electrical process invented almost simultaneously by Paul Heroult, a French metallurgist, and Charles Hall, an American chemist. Find out more about this process that provides us with an abundant supply of low-cost aluminum. What materials are needed? Why is it such an inexpensive process?

16 Chromatography: A Separating Process

The color of many things is actually a combination of color pigments. When the pigments are physically mixed together, but their atoms and molecules are not combined, the different pigments can often be separated. The separation of the pigments is achieved by a process called chromatography.

In this project, you will test different methods of chromatography. You will also determine the effects of various absorbencies of materials on color separation and measure the flow rate of color pigments.

Getting Started

Purpose: To calculate the flow rate for a yellow food dye.

Materials

color-coated candies (such as M&Ms™)

baby-food jar

distilled water

marking pen

masking tape

scissors

ruler

coffee filter

pencil

toothpick

drinking straw

drinking glass

paper clip

water

2-liter plastic soda bottle with cap

Procedure

1. Place ten yellow-colored candies in the baby-food jar.

2. Add enough distilled water to cover the candies.

3. Gently shake the jar until the yellow color on each candy is removed. Dissolve as little of the white undercoating on the candies as possible.

4. Remove and discard these candies. Keep the yellow liquid.

5. Add ten more yellow-colored candies to the yellow liquid in the jar.

6. Again, gently shake the jar until the yellow color on each candy is gone. Remove and discard these candies. Keep the yellow liquid.

7. With the marking pen, write "Yellow Food Dye" on a piece of masking tape and tape this label to the jar.

8. Cut a strip about 1½ inches (3.8 cm) wide and 6 inches (15 cm) long from the coffee filter.

9. Cut a point at one end of the paper strip.

10. Draw a faint pencil line across the pointed end of the paper strip. Use the pencil to label the line "Start."

11. Draw a second pencil line 4 inches (10 cm) above the Start line. Label this second line "End."

12. With the end of the toothpick, transfer a drop of the yellow dye to the center of the start line.

13. Allow the dot of dye to dry before depositing another drop of dye on the same spot.

14. Place ten more drops of dye on the same spot, but allow each dot to dry before adding a new one. *Note:* You want a dark, heavy coating of the yellow pigment on the paper strip.

15. Wrap the even end of the paper strip around the straw.

16. Place the pointed end of the paper strip into the empty glass. Adjust the paper strip so that the point barely touches the bottom of the glass when the straw is resting across the top of the glass.

17. Paper clip the strip around the straw (see Figure 16.1).

18. Remove the strip from the empty glass.

19. Pour water into the glass to a depth of ½ inch (1.8 cm).

20. Return the paper strip to the glass, resting the straw across the top of the glass. *Note:* The point of the paper strip should touch the water, but the yellow dot must be above the water level.

21. Cut off the bottom of the plastic soda bottle.

22. Secure the cap on the bottle and set the bottle over the glass with the paper strip (see Figure 16.2).

23. Watch the water rise up the paper strip. At the instant the water reaches the top line, remove the strip and allow it to dry.

24. Measure the distance from the start line to the center of the color band formed.

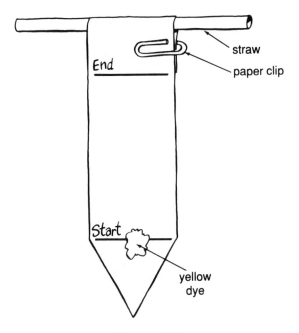

Figure 16.1

25. Use the following equation to calculate the flow rate (R) for the yellow dye. See Appendix 9 for an example calculation.

$$R = \frac{D_1 \text{ (distance the solute travels)}}{D_2 \text{ (distance the solvent travels)}}$$

Results

Yellow streaks of color form and move with the water as it rises up the paper strip. A band of yellow forms on the upper portion of the paper strip below the top line made by the water. The R value for the yellow candy used by the author was 0.65. *Note:* The flow rate (R) will depend on the yellow dye in the brand of candy used.

Why?

Chromatography is a process of separating mixtures by encouraging different parts of the mixture to move through an absorbing material at different rates. Each separated part of the mixture can be identified by its color and flow rate (R). The separation is due to **capillary action** (the rising of the surface of a liquid in small tubes) and solubility.

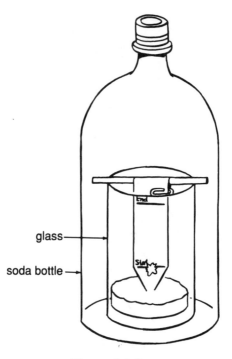

glass—

soda bottle →

Figure 16.2

In this experiment, the tiny fibers in the paper have space between them and form tubelike structures throughout the paper. The solvent, water in this case, is drawn into the fiber tubes and rises due to adhesive and cohesive forces. **Adhesion** is the attraction that the water molecules have for the paper. **Cohesion** is the attraction that the water molecules have for one another. The liquid surface within the spaces is not flat but slightly crescent-shaped, because the adhesion of the water to the paper is greater than the cohesion between the water molecules.

The adhesive attraction of the water to the paper is strong enough to move the water up the sides of the fiber tubes against the downward pull of gravity. The water molecules clinging to the fiber tubes then pull the lower water molecules up the center of the tubes. As the water pulls itself upward, it carries the yellow food dye with it. The distance the dye travels is determined by the attraction it has for water versus its attraction for the paper. The pull of gravity and the attraction to the paper pull the dye molecules out of the water and deposit them on the paper. The color pattern produced on the paper strip is called a **chromatogram.**

Try New Approaches

1. Is the flow rate the same for other colors of food dye?

    a. Repeat the experiment using other candy colors. Some of the colors are a combination of colors. For example, green is made of the primary colors of blue and yellow, and orange is a combination of red and yellow. Determine the flow rate (R) for each color.

    b. Repeat the original experiment using a mixture of the different colors. Calculate the flow rate (R) for each color band on the chromatogram and compare with those calculated for each individual candy color. **Science Fair Hint:** Display the chromatogram and calculated flow rate for each color band.

2. Does the absorbency of the filter paper affect the flow rate? Repeat the original experiment using different types of paper, such as the white edge on newspaper, chromatography paper obtained from your science teacher, and paper towels.

Design Your Own Experiment

1. Is the order of the separating solutes different if the solvent flows down instead of up? Cut a 2-inch (5-cm) strip from a paper towel. Using black water-soluble ink, draw a line across the strip about 4 inches (10 cm) from one end. Set a bowl full of water on a counter next to a sink. Place the end of the paper strip nearest the black line in the bowl of water. Do not let the black line touch the water in the bowl. Allow the strip to hang over the edge of the bowl into the sink (see Figure 16.3). Compare the chromatogram produced in this manner with those previously formed. Display the chromatograms and indicate the procedure by which they were produced.

2. Prepare a leaf chromatogram by laying a geranium leaf, face down, on a round coffee filter. Rub the edge of a coin back and forth over the leaf to produce a green spot about 1 inch (2.5 cm) from the rounded edge of the filter paper. Allow the green spot on the paper to dry before repeating the process. *Note:* You want to collect enough pigment from the leaf to make a dark green spot on the paper. Fold the paper in half twice and secure it with a paper clip. Pour a small amount of rubbing alcohol into a saucer. **CAUTION:** Keep the alcohol away from your nose and mouth. Place the rounded edge of the paper cone in the alcohol. To prevent the alcohol from evaporating too quickly, cover the

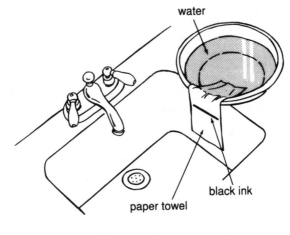

Figure 16.3

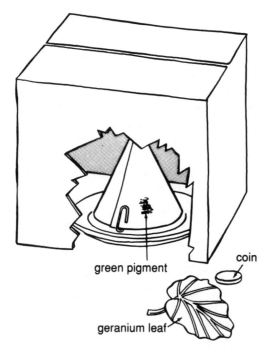

Figure 16.4

paper and saucer with a box (see Figure 16.4). Allow the paper to sit undisturbed for 30 minutes. Display the dry chromatogram.

Get the Facts

1. Plants have a green color because of a pigment called *chlorophyll*. Use a biology text to find out more about plant color pigments. Use this information to identify the colors on the leaf chromatogram.

2. Chromatography is used in industrial plants to separate and measure solutes. Use chemistry texts to find out more about the process of chromatography. What types of absorbents are used other than filter paper? Explain the process of gas chromatography.

17 Coloring and Colorfastness: The Art of Dyeing

For thousands of years, dyes have been used to improve the appearance of things. Our world is filled with beautiful objects that come in all colors of the rainbow.

In this project, you will learn about different methods of preparing material that is to be dyed. You will also determine the colorfastness of dyed fabric and examine the oxidation resulting from bleach and sunlight.

Getting Started

Purpose: To determine whether vinegar is necessary for dyeing eggshells.

Materials

1-pint (500-ml) jar

distilled water

1-teaspoon (5-ml) measuring spoon

blue food coloring

2 cups

marking pen

masking tape

white vinegar (5%)

large spoon

2 eggs (hard-boiled)

paper towel

Procedure

1. Fill the jar half full with distilled water.

2. Add 2 teaspoons (10 ml) of food coloring to the water and stir.

3. Pour half of the colored water into one cup and half into the other.

4. With the marking pen, write "With Vinegar" on a piece of masking tape and tape this label to one cup.

5. Add 1 teaspoon (5 ml) of vinegar to this cup and stir.

6. Label the other cup "Without Vinegar."

105

Figure 17.1

7. Use the large spoon to place one egg in each of the cups (see Figure 17.1).

8. Allow the eggs to remain undisturbed for two minutes.

9. Remove the eggs and place them on a paper towel. Do not dry the eggs with the towel; allow them to air dry.

10. Observe the color of each egg.

Results

The egg soaked in the dye solution containing vinegar is a darker blue than the egg soaked in the dye solution without vinegar.

Why?

To dye an object, the molecules of dye must stick to the surface of the object. In this experiment, the dye is attracted to the eggshell due to a difference between the electrical charge of the molecules of dye and the electrical charge of the molecules on the outside of the eggshell. Vinegar (acetic acid and water) reacts with the layer of protein molecules covering the surface of the eggshell so that the surface becomes positively charged and attracts the negatively charged dye molecules. Some of the dye molecules simply become lodged in crevices in the eggshell; thus, the egg in the solution without vinegar has some color.

Try New Approaches

1. Is the intensity of the color of the egg affected by the concentration of vinegar in the dye solution? Repeat the experiment two times, first adding 2 teaspoons (10 ml) of vinegar to the colored water, and then adding ½ teaspoon (2.5 ml) of vinegar.

2. Does the temperature of the solution affect the results? Repeat the original experiment two times, first adding ice to the colored water to chill it, and then using hot tap water.

3. Does the color of the dye affect the results? Repeat the original experiment using other food colorings. **Science Fair Hint:** Display color photographs of each egg along with descriptions of each procedure.

Design Your Own Experiment

1. Can the surface under the cuticle, the thin protein layer covering the eggshell, be dyed? Use a nail file to rub back and forth across one spot on the surface of a hard-boiled egg until the outer layer of the shell is removed. Fill a cup half full with distilled water. Add 1 teaspoon (5 ml) of red food coloring and 1 teaspoon (5 ml) of vinegar and stir. Place the egg in the red vinegar solution. Remove the egg after two minutes and observe the coloring on and around the area rubbed with the file.

2. Two methods are commonly used to dye cloth. One is **direct dyeing** (dye is affixed directly to the cloth), and the other is **indirect dyeing** (dye unites with a **mordant,** a substance affixed to the surface of the cloth). *Note:* Before demonstrating these two dyeing methods, remove the **sizing** if the material is new (material used to fill the pores of fibers of fabric) from two 12-×-12-inches (30-×-30-cm) pieces of white cotton cloth. Pour 1 cup (250 ml) of water into a saucepan. Add 1 tablespoon (15 ml) of sodium carbonate (washing soda) and stir. Put the cloth pieces in the solution and bring to a boil. Boil for two minutes. Allow the solution to cool. Remove the cloth pieces and rinse in water. Prepare a commercial cloth dye by following the directions on the package. Use the following instructions to dye the cloth pieces.

    a. Direct dyeing can be done by pouring 1 cup (250 ml) of the dye solution into a bowl. Put one of the cloth pieces in the bowl and stir for two minutes. Remove the cloth and rinse with water. Allow the cloth to dry.

sunlight

Figure 17.2

b. Indirect dyeing requires further preparation of the cloth. First, boil the cloth for two minutes in a solution made of 1 cup (250 ml) of water and 1 tablespoon (15 ml) of Epsom salts. After cooling, rinse the cloth with water and soak the cloth in household ammonia for one minute. **CAUTION:** Ammonia is a poison. It and its fumes can damage skin and mucous membranes of nose, mouth, and eyes. Remove the cloth and rinse with water. Wring out any excess water. Soak the cloth in 1 cup (250 ml) of dye solution for two minutes. Remove the cloth and rinse with water. Allow the cloth to dry.

3a. Colorfastness is the resistance a dye has to fading. The oxidation (combining with oxygen) of dye molecules results in molecules that are colorless or that have very little color. Ultraviolet light from the

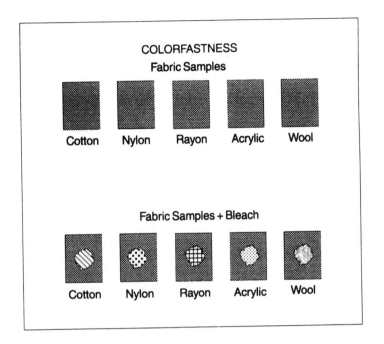

Figure 17.3

sun makes oxygen molecules in the air more reactive; thus, colored materials placed in the sun fade more quickly.

Demonstrate the fading effect of sunlight by folding a piece of red construction paper back and forth into accordionlike pleats (see Figure 17.2). Place the folded paper in a sunny window for four to five days. *Note:* Do not change the position of the paper. Then, unfold the paper and observe the color of the pleats.

b. Bleach contains sodium hypochlorite, a chemical that contains chlorine and oxygen, among other elements. Chlorine has a strong affinity for hydrogen. When bleach comes into contact with a dye containing hydrogen, the hydrogen is removed by the chlorine and oxygen is left in its place. The oxide formed is white or less colored. **CAUTION:** Avoid contact with bleach. It will irritate eyes, skin, and mucous membranes. Do not mix it with acids, ammonia, or other household chemicals because toxic gas may form.

Demonstrate the bleaching effect by adding drops of bleach to a variety of fabric samples including cotton, nylon, rayon, acrylic, and wool that are all of the same color (the colors may not be exact, but make an effort to get them as close as possible). Cut each fabric sample into two 4-inch (10-cm) squares. Place one square of each fabric on a plastic tray and drop three drops of bleach in the center of each piece of fabric. Make observations every ten minutes for one hour. Compare the color of the bleached and unbleached samples. Compare the colorfastness of the different types of fabrics. Rinse the bleached samples with water. Use them on a project display to represent the results (see Figure 17.3).

Get the Facts

1. As long ago as 3000 B.C., dyes extracted from plants were used in China and the Middle East to color textiles. Find out more about natural dyes. Make a list of common plants that can be used to produce specific colors. Discover methods of extracting the dye from plants. You could color pieces of cloth with your dyes and display them.

2. In 1856, the English chemist, William H. Perkin, was trying to produce quinine from coal tar, when he discovered mauve-purple dye. He later discovered a second synthetic dye, magenta. Find out more about synthetic dyes. What contribution did Karl Grabe and Karl Liebermann make to the dye industry? What effect did their discovery have on the profitable cultivation of madder plants in France, Holland, Italy, and Turkey?

18

Viscosity: A Difference in Stickiness

Liquids move to fill up the space of their containers. This ability to move or flow is a very important physical property of liquids. Viscosity is the measurement of the resistance of fluids to flow.

In this project, you will use the viscosity of common household liquids to make a viscometer, an instrument that measures the flow rate of liquids. The flow rate will be used to calculate the viscosity index, the viscosity of a fluid relative to the viscosity of water, of each testing liquid. You will also determine the effect of temperature on viscosity and look at the binding forces between liquid molecules.

Getting Started

Purpose: To make and use a viscometer to determine the flow rate for a defined volume of water.

Materials

scissors

clear plastic dish detergent bottle with a pull top

marking pen

ruler

modeling clay

glass jar with a mouth slightly smaller than the upper part of the detergent bottle

water

timer

Procedure

1. Cut off the bottom of the detergent bottle.
2. Hold the bottle upside down. With the marking pen, make two straight lines, one about 1 inch (2.5 cm) below the cut-off bottom and the second 4 inches (10 cm) below the first line.
3. Label the first line "Start" and the second line "Stop."
4. Close the pull top.

111

5. Place a ring of clay around the top edge of the jar's mouth.

6. Stand the bottle upside down inside the jar. Mold the clay ring so that the bottle stands upright, but do not secure the bottle with the clay.

7. Fill the bottle to about ½ inch (1.3 cm) above the start line with cold tap water.

8. Lift the bottle and pull the top open.

9. Immediately set the bottle back on the jar (see Figure 18.1).

10. Start the timer when the water level reaches the start line.

11. Stop the timer when the water level reaches the stop line.

12. Repeat the procedure three times and average the flow rate of the cold water.

Results

The author's flow rate for cold water was 39.3 seconds. *Note:* The flow rate will vary depending on the bottle used.

Why?

The amount of time it takes a liquid to flow out of a container depends on its viscosity. The viscosity of a liquid is the resistance of the liquid to flowing, because of the friction between the molecules. Viscosity depends on the structure of the liquid molecules. If the molecules are small and simple in structure, as in water, they move past one another quickly. But if they are large and intertwined, as in oil for example, they move slowly past one another. Liquid molecules that slide quickly past one another have a low viscosity; liquid molecules that move more slowly have a high viscosity.

Try New Approaches

1. Does the temperature of water affect its viscosity? Repeat the experiment twice, first chilling the water in a freezer until its temperature is just above the freezing point, and then using warm tap water.

2. How does the viscosity of other liquids compare with the viscosity of water? The flow or viscosity of a liquid compared with the flow of water gives a relative viscosity for the liquid. A number measurement for the relative viscosity of a liquid is called its **viscosity index.** Any number less than 1 indicates a lower viscosity than water; a number greater than 1 indicates a higher viscosity than water. Repeat the orig-

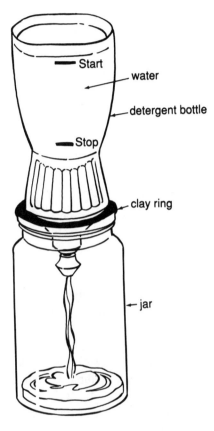

Figure 18.1   Viscometer

inal experiment using liquids such as oil, dishwashing liquid, honey, and/or syrup. Wipe out the viscometer after each test with a paper towel or prepare separate instruments for each liquid tested. Use the flow rate measurements and the following equation to compute the viscosity index for each liquid. See Appendix 10 for an example calculation.

$$\text{viscosity index} = \frac{\text{flow rate of liquid}}{\text{flow rate of water}}$$

Science Fair Hint: Label and display, in order of viscosity index, photographs of each liquid as it flows from the viscometer.

3a. The viscosity of motor oil is rated by the Society of Automotive Engineers (SAE). The numbers assigned are called "weights" and are not exact viscosity values. Do higher weights of oil indicate a more viscous liquid? Repeat the original experiment using light, medium, and heavy weights of motor oil.

b. How does temperature affect the viscosity of oil? Vary the temperature of the motor oil previously tested and again use the viscometer to determine its flow rate. Place some samples in a freezer overnight to chill the oil. Heat other samples by placing containers of oil in hot tap water. Use a thermometer to determine the exact temperature of each sample tested.

Science Fair Hint: Construct and display a graph showing the relationship between temperature and flow rate.

Design Your Own Experiment

1a. Compare the viscosity of liquids by dropping a glass marble into samples of the liquids. Fill identical slender jars with equal amounts of the liquids. Position the jars in front of a white background to increase your ability to clearly see the results. As you observe the contents of the jars, ask a helper to test two liquids at a time by holding a glass marble in each hand, and holding one hand over each jar. The helper should release both marbles from the same height and at the same time. Observe the movement of the marbles through the liquids. Continue to compare two liquids at a time until you can put the liquids in order of viscosity.

b. Vary the temperature of the liquids. Prepare two jars of each testing sample. Chill one in a refrigerator and heat the second by setting it in a bowl of hot tap water. Measure and record the temperature of each liquid and then repeat the experiment. You could display drawings or photographs of the jars, showing them in order of viscosity.

c. Does the viscosity of a liquid affect its stickiness? Test the stickiness of each liquid by dipping your index finger into each liquid one at a time. Touch your thumb and wet index finger together and then slowly separate them. The more difficult it is for you to separate your fingers, the stickier the liquid.

2. Lubricants should be able to be spread on a surface but not run off it. Compare the viscosity of body lubricants such as baby oils, hand

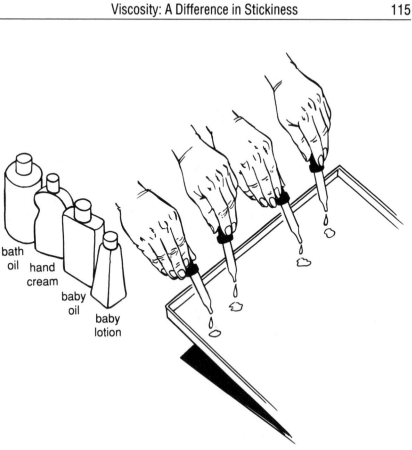

Figure 18.2

creams, and other body lotions by placing drops of the liquids at the top of a cookie sheet raised at one end by a clump of modeling clay. With the assistance of a helper, start the drops of liquid on their downhill flow at the same time (see Figure 18.2). Observe and compare the flow rates of the flowing liquids.

Get the Facts

1. Liquid molecules are free to slide over and around one another. The degree to which these molecules move is directly related to the forces of attraction between the molecules. These forces are called *cohesive forces*. Find out more about this binding force between liquid molecules.

2. What happens to the *kinetic energy* (energy of motion) of molecules in liquids as the temperature is raised? How does this energy affect the binding forces between the molecules? Use this information to explain the effect of temperature on the viscosity of liquids.

3. Find out more about how the Society of Automotive Engineers (SAE) grades motor oil. Is there a difference between oil labeled SAE 30 and oil labeled SAE 30W? What does the label 10–W–30 mean? If temperature affects the viscosity of oil, why is it not necessary to change the oil in a car as the seasons change? This information can be found in some chemistry texts, but a good resource is an automotive mechanic.

19 Crystals: Nature's Jewels

Crystals come in different sizes, shapes, and colors. Some, such as diamonds, are more coveted than others, but they all have their own quality of beauty. By definition, crystals are solids bound by flat surfaces evenly and regularly arranged. Most solids are crystalline, even though their external shapes do not always indicate their orderly internal patterns.

In this project, you will grow crystals that exhibit external structures characteristic of crystals. You will also test the effect of temperature, evaporation rate, and purity of the solution on crystal formation.

Getting started

Purpose: To grow sucrose crystals in a gelatin solution.

Materials:

½ cup (125 ml) of distilled water

small saucepan

0.25 ounce (7-g) of unflavored gelatin

spoon

stove

1-¼ cups (313 ml) of table sugar (sucrose)

1-pint (500-ml) glass jar

Procedure

1. Pour the water into the saucepan.
2. Sprinkle the gelatin on the surface of the water and let it stand undisturbed for two minutes.
3. Stir the liquid continuously over medium heat until the gelatin is completely dissolved.
4. Add the sugar slowly while stirring.
5. Continue to stir until all of the sugar is dissolved.
6. Remove the saucepan from the heat when the liquid starts to boil.
7. Allow the solution to cool for five minutes.
8. Pour the cooled solution into the jar.

9. Place the jar where it can remain undisturbed for two weeks.

10. Make daily observations of the contents of the jar.

Results

The liquid gels when it reaches room temperature. After two or three days, tiny, clear, glistening **crystals** appear suspended throughout the gel (see Figure 19.1). The crystals grow larger each day and form white, feathery, cloudlike clumps throughout the gel.

Why?

Solutions contain a solute (what is dissolved) and a **solvent** (what a solute dissolves in). More solute will dissolve in a hot solvent than would dissolve in a cool solvent. In this experiment, extra sugar is dissolved in the water by heating the water. As the solution cools, more solute is dissolved in the solvent than would normally dissolve at the cooler temperature. This cooled solution with excess solute is called a **supersaturated** solution.

As water evaporates from the solution, the solution becomes even more supersaturated. Supersaturated solutions are unstable, and disturbances will cause the microscopic molecules of solute to stick together and form large, visible crystals. The solute is said to "fall out of solution" when the crystals of solute appear in the solution. The first crystals that fall out of solution are too small to be seen, but as more molecules leave the solution, they bind together and form larger and larger crystals. The gel in this experiment allows the crystals to stay suspended; thus, many clusters of crystals can form.

Try New Approaches

1. Will the crystals continue to grow? Observe the size of the crystals in the jar over a two-month period. **Science Fair Hint:** Make weekly observations and draw diagrams of the crystals. Display the diagrams along with photographs.

2. Crystalline particles arrange themselves in positions that require the least amount of energy for their formation. Crystals are able to do this if they form slowly. The slower the crystal forms, the larger and more perfect is its shape.

    a. Do crystals form more slowly if the supersaturated solution cools slowly? Is there a difference in the sugar crystal formation if the

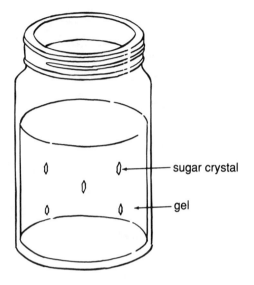

Figure 19.1

solution is cooled at a slower rate by insulating the jar? Repeat the experiment placing the jar inside a large, insulated thermos. Compare the crystals formed in this experiment with those formed in the original experiment.

b. Does evaporation rate affect the speed at which crystals are formed? Repeat the original experiment placing the solution in a small-mouthed bottle, such as a soda bottle. The smaller mouth of the bottle slows the evaporation rate of the water from the solution.

3a. Does the gel alter the shape of the sugar crystals? Repeat the original experiment omitting the unflavored gelatin. Tie a paper clip to the end of a cotton string. Cut the string so that it is just long enough to be attached to a pencil and hung inside the jar with the paper clip resting on the bottom of the jar (see Figure 19.2).

b. Repeat this experiment testing the effect that slow cooling has on crystal growth by placing the jar of hot liquid inside a thermos bottle.

c. Determine whether the rate of evaporation affects the growth of crystals in this watery solution. Repeat this experiment and, as before, use a soda bottle to reduce the exposed surface area of the liquid, thus reducing the rate of evaporation.

Figure 19.2

Design Your Own Experiment

1a. Will sugar crystals form from a solution containing a mixture of different-shaped sugar molecules? Heating a sucrose solution to a high temperature results in the breakdown of some of the sucrose molecules into the smaller sugar molecules of glucose and fructose. An acid, such as cream of tartar, speeds up this breakdown.

    Determine whether sugar crystals will grow in a mixture of glucose, fructose, and sucrose by adding together 1-¼ cups (313 ml) of sugar, 1 teaspoon (5 ml) of cream of tartar, and ½ cup (125 ml) of distilled water. Place the mixture in a small saucepan and heat to boiling while stirring continuously. Boil for five minutes. Cool to room temperature before pouring into a clean soda bottle. Hang a cotton string in the bottle, as was done in a previous experiment. Place the bottle where it can remain undisturbed for two or more weeks. Make daily observations of the contents of the bottle.

b. Another method of testing the crystal growth in a solution of different-shaped sugar molecules is to repeat this experiment replacing the sugar and cream of tartar with 1 cup (250 ml) of sugar and ¼ cup (63 ml) of white corn syrup.

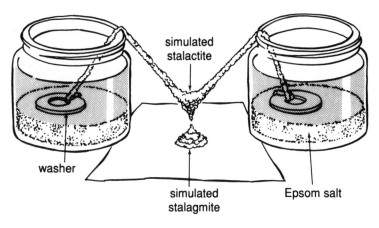

simulated
stalactite

washer

simulated   Epsom salt
stalagmite

Figure 19.3

c. Honey often has white corn syrup added to it to prevent **sugaring** (sugar crystal formation). If pure honey is available, test the effect of sugaring of the honey with and without the addition of white corn syrup. How much corn syrup is needed to prevent sugaring? Increase the speed of the sugaring of the honey by placing it in a refrigerator.

2. Are all crystal shapes the same? Grow crystals from supersaturated solutions containing solutes such as table salt, rock salt, alum, and/ or Epsom salt.

3. How do the crystalline **stalagmites** (formations growing up from the floor) and **stalactites** (deposits hanging from the ceiling) form in caves? Simulate the formation of these structures by filling two baby food jars with Epsom salt. Add water to cover the Epsom salt in each jar and stir. Cut a cotton string 12 inches (30 cm) long and tie a washer on each end. Set the jars on a cookie sheet and place one washer in each jar. Position the jars so that the string hangs between them with the lowest part about 1 inch (2.5 cm) above the cookie sheet (see Figure 19.3). Allow the jars to stand undisturbed and out of any draft for one week. You can use pictures of the development of the formations as part of a project display. Information about the chemical reactions involved in these formations can be found in an experiment called "Fake" (p. 30) in Janice VanCleave's *Earth Science for Every Kid* (New York: Wiley, 1991) and in other earth science texts.

Get the Facts

1. The smallest portion of a crystal is called a *unit cell*. Use a chemistry text to find the shapes of the seven basic unit cell structures. Inexpensive samples of crystals representing the different cell structures can be purchased at rock and mineral shops and displayed along with diagrams of the crystalline systems.

2. What binding forces keep crystals together? Every crystal can be classified by one of four types of lattice structures: ionic, covalent network, metallic, or covalent molecular. Use a chemistry text to find descriptions of the binding forces for each classification. Describe the forces in each and, by means of a chart, represent crystal examples of each type of lattice structure.

3. What type of crystals are found in rocks? Do all rocks contain crystals? Crystals are formed when *magma* (hot, liquid rock) cools. How does the cooling rate of magma affect the type of crystal formed? Use an earth science text to find the answers to these questions and to discover more about crystals formed in nature.

20 Floating: A Chemical Phenomenon

Insects and boats can be seen skimming over the surface of a pond. Different chemical phenomena, including density, buoyancy, and surface tension, explain the floating and sinking of objects.

In this project, you will determine why objects float on water. You will also look at the effect of solutes on the buoyancy and surface tension of water.

Getting Started

Purpose: To determine why objects float on water.

Materials

2-quart (2-liter) bowl
water

modeling clay

Procedure

1. Fill the bowl three-fourths full with cold tap water.
2. Separate two walnut-size pieces of clay. *Note:* The pieces should be of equal size.
3. Roll one of the clay pieces into a ball.
4. Carefully place the clay ball on the surface of the water in the bowl (see Figure 20.1).
5. Observe and record the results.
6. Remove the clay ball from the water and set it aside.
7. Take the second piece of clay and press it into a thin, 3-inch (7.6-cm) square.
8. Turn up about ½ inch (1.3 cm) of each edge to form an open box.
9. Gently place the clay box, open side up, on the surface of the water in the bowl (see Figure 20.2).
10. Observe and record the results.

Figure 20.1

Results

The clay ball sinks in the water. The same amount of clay, when formed into the shape of a box, floats on the surface of the water.

Why?

The mass and thus the weight of the equal-size pieces of clay are the same. Therefore, the sinking of one clay piece and the floating of the other are not dependent on weight. Clay, like all matter, occupies space and therefore has volume. The clay pieces have the same weight but not the same volume. The explanation of the seemingly paradoxical behavior of the clay can be explained by comparing the density and buoyancy of the two pieces.

Density is a comparison of the mass and volume of substances and, in the scientific community, is commonly measured in units of grams per milliliter (cubic centimeter). The density of a substance is calculated by the following formula:

$$\text{density} = \frac{\text{mass}}{\text{volume}}$$

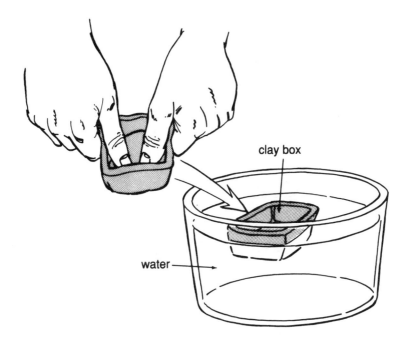

Figure 20.2

The density of water is 1 g/ml and is used as a standard for density measurements. Substances with a density greater than 1 g/ml sink in water; objects with a density less than 1 g/ml float in water. When placed in water, an object **displaces** (pushes aside) the water. Floating objects weigh less than the volume of water that they displace, and sinking objects weigh more than the volume of water that they displace. The weight of the water displaced by an object is equal to the **buoyant force** (amount of upward force) exerted by the water on the object.

The open clay box floats because it takes up more space than the clay ball of equal weight; thus, it has a lower density. The larger-size clay box displaces more water, making it more buoyant than the smaller clay ball of equal weight.

Try New Approaches

How much difference is there between the density of the clay ball and that of the clay box? Repeat the experiment using a scale to determine the mass of the clay pieces.

With a ruler, determine the height, length, and width of the clay box.

Use the following equation to calculate the volume of the clay box:

volume of a box = length × width × height

Determine the density of the clay box by using its mass and dimensions. See Appendix 11 for example calculations. Record your data in a table such as the one shown here.

Density Data Table for Clay Box	
length	
width	
height	
volume (length × width × height) =	
mass	
density (mass/volume) =	

Use the following equation to determine the volume of the clay ball:

volume = 4/3 × **pi** (3.14) × radius cubed

The radius can be calculated by determining the **circumference** (distance around a sphere) of the clay ball. Measure the circumference of the clay ball by wrapping a string around it and measuring the length of the string with a ruler. Use the following equation to determine the radius:

circumference = 2 × 3.14 × radius

Design a data table and record your measurements of the clay ball in it. See Appendix 11 for example calculations.

Design Your Own Experiment

1. Does the purity of water affect its buoyancy? A **hydrometer** is an instrument used to measure the density of a liquid. This instrument rises and sinks in water depending on the amount of dissolved salt. Construct and demonstrate the buoyancy of a hydrometer in pure water and various concentrations of salty water.

Make a simple hydrometer by cutting a 4-inch (10-cm) section from a drinking straw. With a permanent marking pen, draw lines dividing the length of the straw into ten even sections. Use modeling clay to plug up one end of the straw. Drop two or three steel BBs into the straw. Stand the straw, clay plug down, in a glass of distilled water. Use the lines marked on the straw to determine the height of the straw above the water's surface. Remove the hydrometer from the glass and add 1 teaspoon (5 ml) of salt to the water. Place the hydrometer back in the liquid and determine the height of the straw above the water's surface (see Figure 20.3). Repeat this experiment adding 1 teaspoon (5 ml) of salt each time until a total of 6 teaspoons (30 ml) of salt have been added.

2. Insects do not float on the surface of water; they stand on it due to the phenomenon of surface tension. The surface of all liquids behaves differently than the interior. The molecules within the liquid are at-

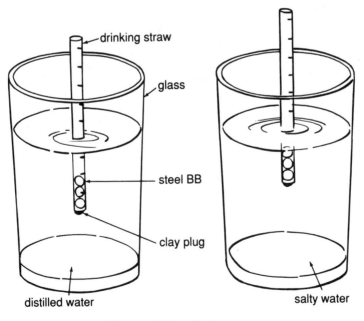

Figure 20.3   Hydrometer

tracted to one another in all directions—sides, top, and below. At the surface, water molecules are attracted only to molecules to their sides and from below.

Since the surface molecules have fewer surrounding molecules, their force of attraction is more focused. Thus, the surface molecules exert a stronger attractive force on the molecules around them, resulting in a strong cohesion among the molecules. The surface molecules are pulled closer together, which produces a skinlike film over the liquid called **surface tension.** Demonstrate the surface tension of water by carefully laying a needle on the surface of water in a bowl. You could display photographs of the experiment along with pictures of insects standing on the surface of water.

Get the Facts

1. Soap and detergents are *surfactants* (substances that accumulate at the surface of a solvent). Surfactants disrupt the surface forces of a liquid and thus decrease its surface tension. Find out more about the effect of surfactants on surface tension. Why do surfactants lower surface tension while solutes, such as sodium chloride, which diffuse homogeneously throughout water, raise the surface tension?

2. The shape of raindrops and water flowing from a faucet are examples of how the force of surface tension pulls the liquid into a shape with the smallest possible surface area. Use chemistry and/or physics texts to find out more about the surface tension of water. What is a *meniscus?* Is it the same in all liquids?

21 Hard Water: A Curdling Problem

Groundwater and water from rivers, streams, and other bodies of water are solutions—mixtures of solvents and solutes. Even the purest of natural water contains some dissolved solutes.

In this project, you will experimentally determine the hardness of water, identify the chemicals responsible for the hardness of water, and learn about methods for softening water. You will also examine the cost-effectiveness of softening water as well as some of the problems hard water can cause.

Getting Started

Purpose: To test for the hardness of water.

Materials

1 tablespoon (15 ml) of distilled water	spoon
	eyedropper
¼ teaspoon (1.2 ml) of Epsom salt	dishwashing liquid
	ruler
baby-food jar with lid	

Procedure

1. Prepare a sample of hard water by combining the distilled water and Epsom salt in the baby-food jar. Stir well.
2. With the eyedropper, add one drop of the dishwashing liquid.
3. Secure the lid on the jar.
4. Shake the jar vigorously for 30 seconds.
5. Allow the jar to stand for 15 seconds.
6. Measure the height of the suds above the water level.
7. Observe and describe the appearance of the suds (see Figure 21.1).

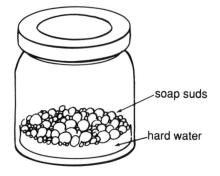

Figure 21.1

Results

Soap suds form above the water. The height of the suds in the jar used by the author was ¼ inch (0.63 cm). *Note:* The height of the suds will depend on the shape of the baby-food jar used.

Why?

The **hardness of water** is a measure of the amount of calcium, magnesium, and/or iron salts dissolved in the water. These cations (positive particles) make it difficult for soap to make suds. They combine with the fatty acid anions (negative particles) in soap to form waxy, insoluble salts. Magnesium sulfate's common name is Epsom salt. The magnesium in the chemical combines with the fatty acid in the dishwashing liquid to form soap scum instead of soap suds.

In areas where the concentration of calcium, magnesium, and/or iron in the water is high, **precipitates** (insoluble molecules that separate from the solution) are deposited around the sides of bathtubs and sinks. The effectiveness of soap is reduced by the minerals in hard water. Much of the soap that would otherwise be used in cleaning combines with the minerals in hard water to form the insoluble salts known as **soap scum** or **soap curd.** The soap scum also sticks to the surface of your skin and hair during bathing and to the surface of clothes when washed, giving the surfaces a slightly sticky, dull appearance.

Try New Approaches

1. How effective is dishwashing liquid in **soft water** (water without calcium, magnesium, and/or iron cations)? Repeat the experiment using distilled water only. If the baby-food jar restricts the height of the suds, use a jar with a comparable diameter, but taller.

2. Compare the hardness of different water samples. Collect water from as many different locations as possible. Test any available rivers, ponds, or streams. Record the height and description of each test in a data table such as the one shown here. **Science Fair Hint:** Mark the height of the suds in each testing jar, take a photograph of each jar, and display the photographs in order of the height of suds.

Data Table		
Water Source	Height of Suds	Description of Suds

3. Soap must first remove the minerals in hard water before it can form suds. Test one water sample at a time to determine how many drops of soap are needed for the water to produce an amount of suds comparable to those formed by the distilled water. Add two drops of dishwashing liquid at a time. Keep a record of the number of drops used. Repeat the procedure for each water sample. **Science Fair Hint:** Construct and display a bar graph showing the results.

4. Water-softening chemicals such as borax (sodium borate) are added to hard water so that soap can work more efficiently. Demonstrate this by repeating the original experiment adding ¼ teaspoon (1.2 ml) of borax to the jar. Shake as before and compare the height of the suds formed with those in the jar without the borax.

5. How soft is the rainwater where you live? Surface water evaporates and becomes a gas, or water vapor. The water vapor condenses and eventually returns to the earth as raindrops. The purity of the water depends on the contaminants in the air. Repeat the original experiment using collected rainwater. Make an effort to collect and test rainwater from different locations.

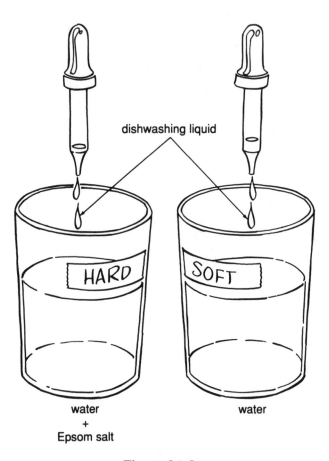

Figure 21.2

Design Your Own Experiment

1a. The clarity of soapy water can be used as an indication of the hardness of water. Demonstrate this by filling two drinking glasses half full with distilled water. Add 1 teaspoon (5 ml) of Epsom salt to one glass and label it "Hard." Label the other glass "Soft." Add 30 drops of dishwashing liquid to each glass and stir (see Figure 21.2). Hold the glasses in front of a light source such as a lamp or an open window. Observe the clarity of each solution.

b. Soap removes magnesium ions from water, thus making the water softer. How much soap is needed to soften the water? Allow the water in the glass labeled "Hard" to sit for several hours. Notice the layer of white powder on the bottom of the glass. **Decant** (pour off) as much of the water from this glass as possible without disturbing the white residue. Add ½ teaspoon (2.5 ml) of liquid soap to this water, stir, and observe the clarity of the water. Continue this process until the water clarity is the same as that of the water in the glass labeled "Soft." Keep count of the total number of soap drops added.

2. Hard water creates problems other than that of increasing the amount of soap needed for cleaning. A chalklike substance, made largely of calcium and magnesium salts, forms hard crusts that can clog hot-water boilers and pipes. Demonstrate the formation of this material, called **boiler scale,** by boiling hard water in a teakettle. Allow the kettle to heat to dryness. Repeat to increase the thickness of the scale. Use the kettle as part of a project display. *Note:* The boiler scale can be removed from the kettle by covering the scale with vinegar and allowing it to soak for several hours.

Get the Facts

1. Use a chemistry text to find the formula for soap. Write the chemical equation for the reaction between one of the ions in hard water (calcium, magnesium, or iron) and the soap molecule. Display this equation to represent the results of adding soap to hard water.

2. Home water-purification systems are available for purchase. Find out more about these systems. Check the telephone yellow pages for a water filtration and purification equipment company in your area. Some purifiers filter the water through activated charcoal, while others deionize the water. Which process produces soft water? Is it more cost-effective to purchase a purification unit or simply to add more soap?

22 Molecular Motion: A Matter of Energy

Matter is anything that takes up space and has weight. It appears to be made of minute individual particles, or molecules, which are separated from one another and are in constant motion.

In this project, you will explore the molecular motion of matter as you determine why a fish smells "fishy" and what effect lemon juice has in reducing the smell. You will also examine the effect of temperature on molecular motion and the difference in molecular motion among the different phases of matter, and you will experiment with a "non-Newtonian" fluid.

Getting Started

Purpose: To determine whether lemon juice reduces the fishy smell of fish.

Materials

3 cups

water

4 tablespoons (60 ml) of lemon juice

spoon

marking pen

masking tape

3 pieces of uncooked fish about 2 inches (5 cm) square

dark scarf (large enough to be a blindfold)

helpers (as many as possible)

3 forks

Procedure

1. Fill two of the cups half full with cold tap water.

2. Add 4 tablespoons (60 ml) of lemon juice to the water in only one of the cups and stir.

3. With the marking pen, write "Air," "Water," and "Lemon" on pieces of masking tape and tape these labels to the appropriate cups.

135

4. Place a piece of fish in each of the cups.

5. Allow the fish to remain in the cups for 15 minutes.

6. Blindfold one helper with the scarf.

7. Use one of the forks to remove the fish from the mixture of lemon juice and water.

8. Hold the lemon-soaked fish near, but not touching, the nose of the blindfolded helper.

9. Ask your helper to smell the fish and make a mental note of its smell.

10. Repeat the procedure twice with the same helper, first using the fish soaked in water, and then using the fish sitting in air. Use a separate fork each time.

11. Ask your helper to compare the smell of the three pieces of fish (see Figure 22.1).

12. Repeat the entire procedure with each helper.

Results

The fish sitting in air has the strongest fishy smell. The water-soaked fish has less odor, and the lemon-soaked fish has the least odor.

Why?

Olfaction (the sense of smell) is the response of **chemoreceptors** (sensory nerves) to gases that enter the nasal cavity. A material "smells" or has a scent only if it releases gas molecules. The degree or intensity of the scent is due to the concentration of gas that enters the nasal cavity. The specific smell is due to the chemical makeup of the gas molecules. Gas molecules have **translational energy** (energy associated with gas molecules as they move linearly from one point to another). The self-spreading of the gas due to its translational energy is known as **diffusion.**

The fishy smell of fish comes from **amines** (organic chemicals associated with decaying flesh). In the cup filled with air, the amine molecules can escape from the fish and diffuse through the spaces around the air molecules. This increased concentration of amine molecules in the air produces the strong fishy smell.

The water-soaked fish has a reduced odor because the water surrounding the fish restricts the movement of the amine gas into the air and some of the gas molecules also dissolve in the water. Thus, the concentration of fishy-smelling gas in the air is reduced.

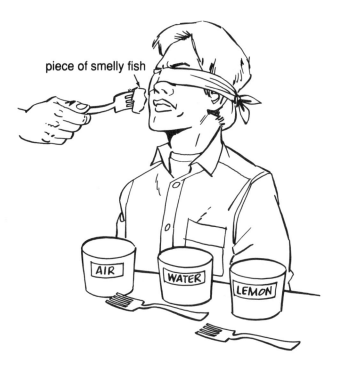

piece of smelly fish

Figure 22.1

The lemon-soaked fish smells the least because many of the amine molecules are chemically changed before they have time to vaporize. Amines behave as bases, and lemon juice is an acid. Like all bases, amines combine with an acid to form a salt. In this reaction, the salt produced does not give off aromatic vapor; thus, the fishy-smelling amines are chemically eliminated by the addition of lemon juice.

Try New Approaches

Does temperature affect the diffusion of the amine vapor? Repeat the experiment two times, first setting the cups in bowls of ice water, and then placing them in bowls of hot water.

Design Your Own Experiment

1a. Demonstrate the fact that water molecules are in constant motion. Mix together in a 1-quart (1-liter) jar, 1 teaspoon (5 ml) of sodium chloride (table salt), five drops of green food coloring, and 1 cup (250 ml) of water. Tilt the jar and slowly pour a second cup (250 ml) of water down the inside of the jar. The result is a layer of green water covered by a layer of clear water (see Figure 22.2). Place the jar where it can remain undisturbed for three days. Observe the contents of the jar as often as possible. The motion of the water molecules is evident as the two layers start to mix. The end result is a uniformly green-colored liquid.

b. Determine whether temperature affects the molecular motion of the water molecules. Repeat the previous experiment two times, first using chilled water with ice cubes and placing the jar in a refrigerator, and then using hot tap water and placing the jar in a warm area.

2. Molecules rotate about their axes, as does the earth. The rotational energy creating this molecular motion can produce heat. For example, in microwave heating, water in food absorbs the energy waves, or microwaves, causing the individual water molecules to spin like tops. As these molecules twirl, they hit and rub against other water molecules. Rubbing your hands together very quickly demonstrates the ability of friction to produce heat. Predict the effect of microwaves on materials that do not contain water, such as a paper plate. Would the paper get hot? Why?

3. The three **phases of matter**—solid, liquid, and gas—have distinct physical properties because of the differences in their molecular motion. The amount of energy that a substance possesses determines its molecular motion and thus its phase of matter. Molecular motion is directly dependent on energy. As molecular motion decreases, molecules get closer together and the cohesion (attraction between like molecules) increases. Solids have the lowest energy, the least molecular motion, and the greatest cohesion between molecules. Demonstrate the physical changes made by increasing molecular motion by heating ice. You could display diagrams to illustrate the closeness of the molecules in different phases.

4. Gases and liquids are classified as **fluids** because both are able to flow and to change their shapes. Sir Isaac Newton (1642–1727) is credited with stating the relationship between temperature and the viscosity of fluids. This **law of viscosity** states that only a change in temperature affects the viscosity of a fluid. Newton had never seen the "Glob," a creepy ooze that, like other fluids, has an increase in

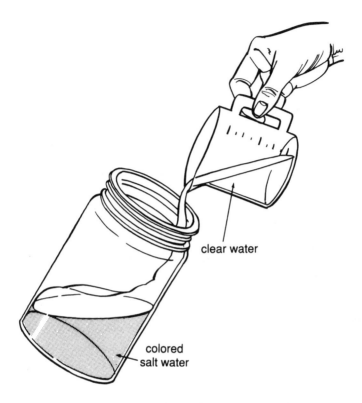

clear water

colored
salt water

Figure 22.2

molecular motion with an increase in temperature but that, unlike other fluids, has its viscosity increase with an increase in pressure. Pressure makes it behave as a solid. Since the Glob defies Newton's law about fluids, it is considered a "non-Newtonian" fluid.

a. Make the Glob by using the following instructions. **CAU-TION:** Keep the Glob out of reach of small children. It is not edible.

- Combine 4 ounces (120 ml) of Elmer's® school glue, 4 ounces (120 ml) of distilled water, and ten drops of green food coloring. Stir well and set aside.

- In a separate bowl, combine 1 teaspoon (5 ml) of sodium borax with 1 cup (250 ml) of distilled water. Stir well.

- Pour both solutions into an empty bowl simultaneously.
- Stir and dip the thick Glob out of the bowl.
- Knead the Glob with your hands until it is smooth and dry.

b. Try the following experiments with the Glob.

- Roll it into a ball and bounce it on a smooth surface.
- Hold it in your hands and quickly pull the ends in opposite directions.
- Hold it in your hands and slowly pull the ends in opposite directions.
- Place a lemon-size piece into a microwave dish and heat for one half minute in a microwave oven. *Note:* Microwave heating will make the Glob too hot to handle. Allow it to stand in the oven for about five minutes so that it returns to room temperature.
- Place a piece in a freezer overnight and then allow it to return to room temperature.

Note: The Glob will keep for weeks in a plastic bag, but after much handling it will dry out.

Get the Facts

1. The continuous movement of molecular particles is called *Brownian movement.* Find out more about the perpetual dancing of molecules and the experiment that led Robert Brown, a Scottish scientist, to discover their motion.

2. The smell of the sea is due to the release of amines by decaying marine life. Because these amines are associated with the decaying flesh of animals, the common names of two amines are *cadaverine* (from "cadaver") and *putrescine* (from "putrefy"). An amine is considered a base as defined by the Bronsted-Lowry theory and by the Lewis theory. Use a chemistry text to find out more about this organic base. What is its general chemical structure? What is its distinguishing chemical makeup? How are amines related to ammonia? Include in your findings the reaction between an amine and an acid.

23 Polymers: Chains of Simple Molecules

Polymers are giant molecules formed by the bonding together of monomers, which are small molecules that link together. These macromolecules are formed naturally and synthetically.

In this project, you will look at how monomers are connected and the organization of the resulting polymeric chains. The effect of linking different types of monomers will be determined. Plastics of different chemical compositions will be experimentally separated by their densities. You will also examine the effect of temperature on vulcanized rubber.

Getting Started

Purpose: To demonstrate that the physical property of a material depends on the way polymeric chains organize themselves.

Materials

5-ounce (150-ml) paper cup	pencil
water	clear plastic sandwich bag
baking pan	

Procedure

1. Fill the paper cup three-fourths full with water.

2. Place the baking pan on a table.

3. Stand the paper cup in the baking pan.

4. Push the pointed end of the pencil through one side of the cup and out the other side. **CAUTION:** Be careful not to stick yourself with the pencil.

5. Leave the pencil in place and observe any leakage around the pencil (see Figure 23.1).

6. Remove the pencil and observe any leakage.

7. Note the size and shape of the hole made by the pencil in the paper cup.

8. Fill the plastic sandwich bag three-fourths full with water.

141

9. Position the bag over the baking pan.

10. While holding the bag at the top, push the pointed end of the pencil through one side of the bag and out the other side.

11. As before, leave the pencil in place and observe any leakage around the pencil (see Figure 23.2).

12. Remove the pencil and observe any leakage.

13. Note the size and shape of the hole made by the pencil in the plastic bag.

Results

The impaled paper cup has small water drops leaking around the pencil where it enters and leaves the cup. Removal of the pencil reveals that the pencil tore the paper and produced a hole with a diameter about the same size as that of the pencil. Water quickly pours out of this hole.

The impaled plastic bag does not leak. Removal of the pencil shows that the hole left by the pencil appears stretched around the edges (not torn) and is slightly smaller in diameter than that of the pencil. Water is able to stream out of this hole.

Why?

Cellulose is the principal component of paper. Cellulose is a polymer (macromolecule formed by the repeated chemical linking of many

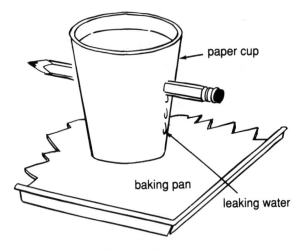

Figure 23.1

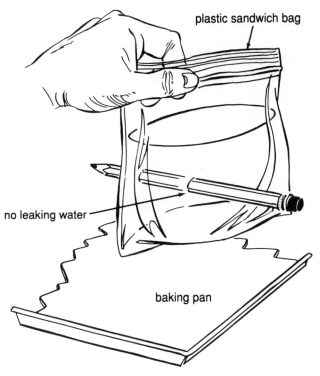

plastic sandwich bag

no leaking water

baking pan

Figure 23.2

smaller molecules called monomers) made by linking hundreds or thousands of glucose molecules together. The clear plastic bag is made of polyethylene. Ethylene is the monomer used to make polyethylene. Like cellulose, polyethylene can contain thousands of monomers.

The physical organization of the polymeric chains of these two macromolecules differs, however. Cellulose is more like a straight chain, and polyethylene is like a ball of fuzzy yarn with fibers intertwined and sticking out in all directions (see Figure 23.3, where the football players representing cellulose are in a straight line and those representing polyethylene are in a big pile). The polyethylene molecules are more attracted to one another and are all entangled.

When the pencil enters the paper cup, the cellulose chains are easily broken. When it enters the plastic bag, the polyethylene molecules move out of the way, remain entangled, and pull together around the pencil. The plastic is prevented from tearing or leaking as long as the pencil remains in place.

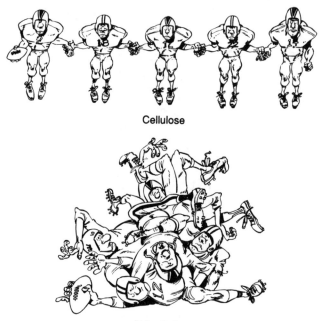

Cellulose

Polyethylene
Figure 23.3

Try New Approaches

1. Does the size of the hole affect the results? Repeat the experiment two times, first using a pencil with a larger diameter, and then using a pin.

2. Does the shape of the hole affect the results? Repeat the original experiment replacing the pencil with a knife. **Science Fair Hint:** Display photographs to represent the procedure and results.

3. Do other polyethylene plastics behave the same way? Use the part of the original experiment that tests the plastic bag to test other plastic samples such as other plastic storage bags, garbage bags, and plastic wraps.

Design Your Own Experiment

1. There are many different kinds of plastics. When recycling, plastics must be chemically similar to be mixed together. One way to sort plastic is by density. Prepare a density-testing solution by mixing together 1 cup (250 ml) of water and 2 cups (500 ml) of rubbing alcohol in a 1-quart (1-liter) jar. Cut two 2-inch (5-cm) squares of plastic, one from a plastic milk bottle and a second from a plastic garbage bag. Drop the two plastic pieces into the mixture of alcohol and water. If both pieces sink, stir in small amounts of water until one piece floats. If both pieces float, stir in small amounts of alcohol until one piece sinks. Use this technique to sort pieces taken from other plastic products.

2a. Rubber is a polymer. Its principle component unit is isoprene. Natural rubber is affected by temperature. It becomes soft and smelly when hot and hard and stiff when chilled. Test the effect of temperature on **vulcanized** rubber, which is chemically treated to increase its strength, hardness, and elasticity. Place a rubber band in a freezer for several hours. Remove it and test for changes in hardness and **elasticity** (ability to return to its original shape after being stretched). Place the rubber band in boiling water for five minutes. Note any change in odor when the material is heated. Carefully remove it with tongs and with protective mitts again test for hardness and elasticity.

b. Rubber cement is a mixture of rubber and a solvent. Is the rubber natural or vulcanized? Brush a thick layer of rubber cement over a 4-×-12-inch (10-×-30-cm) piece of wax paper. Allow the cement to dry. Starting on the long side of the painted section, use your fingers to roll the layer of rubber off the paper. Gently stretch the rubber roll to determine its elasticity. Test the effect of temperature on the rubber as in the previous experiment. Base your conclusion on the effect of temperature on the material.

Get the Facts

1. There are many important natural polymers, such as starch, cellulose, protein, and rubber. By studying these and other natural polymers, chemists are able to reproduce the *polymerization* process to make synthetic polymers such as nylon, plastics, and Teflon®. Find out more about natural and synthetic polymers. What types of plastics are produced and what are their major applications? What is a *homopolymer*? What is the difference between condensation polymers and addition polymers? How do polymers called *elastomers* behave?

2. In natural rubber, the long chains are separate and can move past one another, but the *vulcanization* process causes sulfur bridges to form between the chains like rungs on a ladder. How does the vulcanization process affect the physical properties of rubber? Find out more about natural, vulcanized, and synthetic rubber. Discover the circumstances of Charles Goodyear's serendipitous discovery of vulcanization. What is the source of natural rubber? How is it collected? How is it processed?

3. In 1909, the first fully synthetic polymer, Bakelite®, was presented by its discoverer, Leo H. Baekeland. How is this synthetic resin produced? Is it a thermosetting plastic or a thermoplastic? What are the major uses of Bakelite?

4. The two naturally occurring polymers of isoprene are *cis*-polyisoprene (rubber) and *trans*-polyisoprene (gutta-percha). What is the structural difference between these two polymers? How does it affect the physical properties of the materials?

Mega-Absorbers: Osmotically Speaking

24

Makers of disposable diapers claim that their product is superior to cloth diapers because it keeps babies dryer longer. They suggest that their diapers hold more liquid and actually pull the liquid away from a baby's skin.

In this project, you will test these claims and determine the effect of the mega-absorbent polymer, sodium polyacrylate, on the absorbency of materials. You will also compare the absorbency of paper towels and determine why some are so absorbent.

Getting Started

Purpose: To determine the amount of distilled water that a high-absorbency disposable diaper will hold.

Materials

1-×-1-×-1-foot (30-×-30-×-30- cm) cardboard box

scissors

disposable diaper of medium-high absorbency

2 clothespins

cereal bowl

2-cup (500-ml) measuring cup

distilled water

Procedure

1. Remove the top and one side from the box.

2. Use scissors to cut a hole about the size of a quarter in the center of the diaper's plastic outer covering.

3. Drape the diaper, plastic covering down, across the top of the box and secure the ends of the diaper to the top edge of the box with the clothespins.

4. Place the bowl inside the box directly under the hole in the diaper.

5. Fill the measuring cup with distilled water.

6. Slowly pour the water over the inside surface of the diaper from one end to the other (see Figure 24.1).

7. Continue to pour water into the diaper until water begins to drip out the hole cut in the plastic covering and into the bowl.

8. Record the total amount of water poured into the diaper.

Note: Dispose of all diaper material in the trash. Do not put any material down the drain.

Results

The diaper tested by the author held 5 cups of distilled water. *Note:* The amount of water will vary with the brand of diaper used.

Why?

Sodium polyacrylate is a polymer (large, usually chainlike molecule made by combining smaller molecules). It is manufactured by the polymerization (process of joining small molecules to form a large molecule) of a mixture of sodium acrylate and acrylic acid. As water is added, it is immediately absorbed by a process called **gelling.** The ability of the polymer to absorb excessive amounts of water is due to **osmotic pressure** (the movement of water through a membrane permeable only to water). Water moves from an area of high water concentration to an area of lower water concentration. The difference in water concentration between the inside of the polymer and the pure distilled water surrounding it is due to the concentration of **ions** (charged particles, in this case, of sodium and polyacrylate) inside the polymer. The polymer continues to absorb water until an equilibrium is reached where the water concentration inside the polymer equals that of the water solution in which it is immersed.

Try New Approaches

1. A baby's urine has a higher concentration of electrolytes (substances that dissolve, forming ions) than water. Would the electrolyte concentration in the water affect the amount of water absorbed by the polymer? Repeat the experiment two times, first using ordinary water, and then replacing the water with a 0.9% salt solution (use the instructions in Appendix 5 to make the solution) similar to the sodium chloride concentration in urine. **Science Fair Hint:** Display photographs of the diapers, with cups indicating the quantity of each solution that each diaper held.

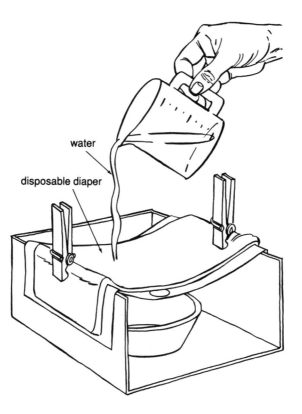

Figure 24.1

2. Do expensive disposable diapers hold more liquid, as their ads claim? Repeat the original experiment using brands of diapers of varying cost. **Science Fair Hint:** Display a chart showing the results of each brand tested.

Design Your Own Experiment

1. Do disposable diapers actually keep a baby dryer? Place a disposable diaper on a cookie sheet and pour 2 cups (500 ml) of water into the diaper. Press the palm of your hand against the surface of the wet diaper. Lift and observe the surface of your hand for any wetness. Repeat the experiment using different brands and compare their effectiveness in keeping wetness away from a baby's skin.

2. Some disposable diapers are advertised as being designed for boys or for girls. Is there a difference in the absorbency of the fiber in different areas of these diapers? Remove the lining and plastic outer covering from two diapers, one designed for boys and one designed for girls. Cut the inner fiber of each diaper into four equal sections. Lay the pieces of fiber from one diaper in a line on a cookie sheet. Do the same with the other diaper fibers on another cookie sheet. Raise both cookie sheets at one end by lemon-size clumps of modeling clay. Use a measuring cup to add distilled water evenly to the surface of each piece of fiber (see Figure 24.2). Measure and record the amount of water that each piece absorbs. Repeat this procedure using different brands of diapers.

3. Sodium polyacrylate is nontoxic, but it will dry and irritate the mucous membranes of the eyes, nose, and mouth. As it combines with water, the sodium polyacrylate in the fiber of a disposable diaper inflates and forms a gel. Addition of table salt causes the gelled polymer to break down as water moves outside the polymer network. Demonstrate this change in texture caused by the movement of water into and out of the polymer. Remove the inside fiber from a diaper. Cut the piece in half and place each piece in a separate 2-quart (2-liter) bowl. Add enough water to totally saturate each piece. Observe the change in size of the fiber as the water is added. Crumble the fiber in both bowls to form a wet mush. Rub the material between your fingers and observe the pieces of gel mixed in with the fiber. Add 2 tablespoons (30 ml) of sodium chloride to one bowl. Mix and, with your hands, examine the texture of the material again (see Figure 24.3). *Note:* Wash your hands to remove the sodium polyacrylate.

4. Polyacrylate is used in products other than high-absorbency diapers. Tour a department store and note products that are designed to absorb moisture, such as plant potting soil and fuel filters for vehicles. You could display the products themselves or pictures of the products containing the polymer.

5. Chemicals aid the absorbency of products, but the physical structure of the product can also increase absorbency. Paper towels vary in their ability to absorb liquids. Compare the texture of different brands of paper towels. Test the absorbency of each brand by immersing a paper towel in a measuring cup filled with water. Lift the towel and determine the amount of water removed from the cup.

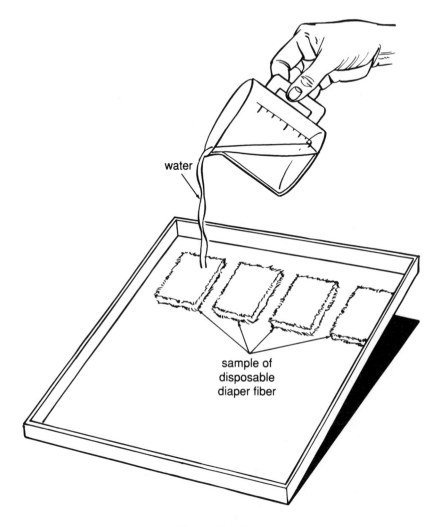

water

sample of
disposable
diaper fiber

Figure 24.2

Get the Facts

1. How much sodium polyacrylate must be used in each diaper? The quantity of the polymer needed to absorb the equivalent amount of water absorbed by a diaper can be experimentally determined. To purchase the pure polymer whose trade name is Waterlock®, consult a current Flinn chemical catalog for price and ordering information or write to Flinn Scientific, Inc., P.O. Box 219, Batavia, IL 60610.

water
+
diaper
+
sodium chloride

SALT

Figure 24.3

2. Paper towels are made of tiny fibers. The spaces between the fibers form tubelike structures through which liquids move. How does the liquid move through the fibers? What is adhesion and how does it affect the paper's absorbency rating? For information about the movement of liquids through a paper towel, see the "Why?" section of "Uphill Climbers" (p. 29) in Janice VanCleave's *Spectacular Science Projects: Molecules* (New York: Wiley, 1992).

25 Water: The Irregular Liquid

Water is a common liquid that often behaves in a most uncommon fashion. It is an exception to some of nature's laws because of its unique properties.

In this project, you will compare the differences and similarities of this unique liquid to other liquids. You will also study the hydrogen bonding in water molecules, which causes many of its irregular, but important properties, such as its expansion when frozen and its cohesiveness.

Getting Started

Purpose: To measure the attractiveness (stickiness) between water molecules.

Materials

3 pencils

duct tape

7-ounce (210-ml) paper cup

scissors

ruler

string

suction cup (type used to secure hanging crafts to windows)

baking pan

2 saucers or plates with smooth, flat bottoms (made of material not easily broken)

3 rolls of pennies

distilled water

Procedure

1. Place one pencil parallel with the edge of a table.

2. Place the second pencil across the first pencil with about 2 inches (5 cm) of its end slightly elevated and extending over the table's edge.

3. Use tape to secure the pencils to the table.

4. Use the third pencil to punch two holes under the rim of the paper cup on opposite sides. **CAUTION:** Be careful not to stick yourself with the pencil.

153

5. Cut an 8-inch (20-cm) length of string.

6. Tie the ends of the string through each hole in the cup to form a loop.

7. Cut a 1-yard (1-m) length of string and attach it to the string loop on the cup.

8. Tie the free end of the string to the hook on the suction cup.

9. Place the baking pan on the floor beneath the hanging string.

10. Turn one saucer upside down and place it in the pan.

11. Set the second saucer on top of the first one so that the bottoms of the saucers are touching.

12. Press the suction cup so that it is secured to the center of the top saucer.

13. Loop the string over the extended pencil and allow the cup to hang freely.

14. Add coins to the cup until the saucers are slightly separated (see Figure 25.1).

15. Count and record the number of coins needed to separate the saucers.

16. Separate the saucers and wet the bottoms of each with the distilled water.

17. Press the saucers together.

18. Again, determine the number of coins needed to separate the saucers.

19. Compare the number of coins needed to separate the dry and wet saucers.

Results

More coins are needed to separate the saucers when they have a layer of water between them than when they are dry.

Why?

The formula for water is H_2O, which means that one molecule of water has two hydrogen atoms bonded to one oxygen atom. The molecule has a bent shape and a positive and a negative side. Molecules like water that have a positive and a negative side are called **polar molecules.** This polarity results in an attraction between water molecules. This attraction is called cohesion and is a result of the positive side of one water molecule

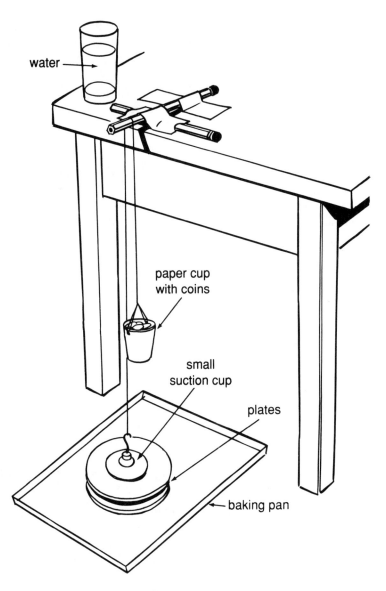

water

paper cup
with coins

small
suction cup

plates

baking pan

Figure 25.1

attracting the negative side of another water molecule. The attraction of water for a different molecule, such as those in the saucers, is called adhesion. The water sticks to the saucers due to adhesive forces, and then the water layers on the saucers stick together by cohesive forces. The number of coins needed to separate the saucers gives an indication of the strength of the cohesive force between water molecules.

Try New Approaches

1. Do solutes affect the cohesiveness of water? Repeat the experiment adding 1 teaspoon (5 ml) of solute to 1 cup (250 ml) of water each time the experiment is performed. Suggested solutes are sucrose (table sugar), sodium chloride (table salt), and dishwashing liquid.

2. Does water have more cohesiveness than other liquids do? Repeat the original experiment using rubbing alcohol. **Science Fair Hint:** Display a model of the instrument used to measure the cohesive force between liquid molecules. Replace the pencils with a hook attached to the top of a board. **CAUTION:** Keep the alcohol away from your nose and mouth.

Design Your Own Experiment

1. Sand sculptures can be made with wet sand because of the adhesion between the sand and water and the cohesion between the water molecules. Use wet sand to form a sculpture in a tray. Take photographs of your artwork before and after gently shaking the tray. Rebuild and allow the sand sculpture to completely dry and then shake the tray again. Take a third photograph. Display your pictures as proof of the adhesive power that water provides between the sand grains.

2. The normal reaction to changes in temperature for most substances is that they expand when heated and contract when cooled. Water contracts when cooled from a warm temperature until it reaches 39.2°F (4°C). At this temperature, water is the most dense because the molecules occupy the least amount of space. As the temperature decreases, the density of water decreases as the molecules move farther apart. At 32°F (0°C), water freezes and occupies the most space (see Figure 25.2). The expansion of the ice structure exerts enough force to break apart rocks when liquid water that has seeped into cracks in the rocks freezes.

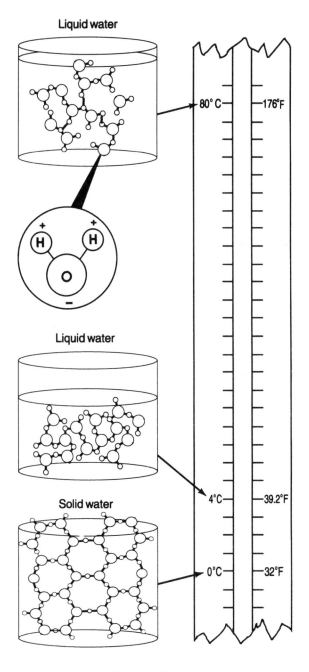

Figure 25.2

Demonstrate this unique behavior of water by filling a plastic soda bottle to overflowing with water. Secure the cap and place the bottle of water in a freezer. After the water has completely frozen, observe the container. *Note:* Do not try this experiment with a glass container. Display diagrams representing the volume of water at different temperatures and drawings or photographs of the soda bottle filled with water before and after freezing. Also display pictures representing the practical results of this water-expanding phenomenon, like the formation of potholes in streets during freezing wet weather.

Get the Facts

1. The bonding between the hydrogen and oxygen atoms in water molecules affects the shape of the molecules as well as their physical and chemical properties. Use a chemistry text to find out more about the covalent and hydrogen bonds in water molecules. The angle between the two hydrogen-to-oxygen bonds is about 105°. How does the sp³ hybridization of the oxygen-atom orbitals create the angle and thus a bent-shaped water molecule? Why are water molecules polar? How do hydrogen bonds account for the values of water's vapor pressure, surface tension, specific heat, and boiling point? How do hydrogen bonds create the phenomenon called *surface tension?*

2. The hydrogen bonding between water molecules results in the linking of four to eight molecules that form liquid water. Ice is the linking of six molecules in an open hexagonal pattern. This rigid lattice structure of ice occupies more space than liquid water does. Find out about the difference in the length of hydrogen bonds between water molecules at different temperatures. How does the length of these bonds affect the flexibility of the connected water molecules?

26 Oxygen: Combined and Free

Oxygen is the most abundant element in the earth's crust and ranks third in abundance in the known universe. It is necessary for the support of plant and animal life.

In this project, you will chemically produce oxygen and test for the presence of the gas. The physical and chemical properties of the gas will be examined. You will also look at the role of plants in the production of oxygen in the atmosphere as well as the corrosive effect of acid rain.

Getting Started

Purpose: To produce and test for the presence of oxygen gas.

Materials

baby-food jar (or other small glass jar)

uncooked ground beef (hamburger meat)

cookie sheet

3% hydrogen peroxide

long, tapered candle

match

Procedure

1. Fill the jar half full with meat.
2. Set the jar in the center of the cookie sheet.
3. Fill the jar with hydrogen peroxide.
4. Hold the candle at the end away from the wick and light the wick with the match.
5. Allow the candle to burn for about 15 seconds, then blow out the flame and insert the glowing wick into one of the larger bubbles that has formed on the surface of the liquid in the jar. *Note:* It is important that the wick be red hot when it touches the wet bubble (see Figure 26.1).
6. Blow out the candle and lay it on the cookie sheet to cool.

Figure 26.1

CAUTION: It is not safe to repeat the experiment with the same candle because the wick becomes ragged and difficult to blow out.

Results: The glowing wick bursts into flame.

Why?

The decomposition of hydrogen peroxide, H_2O_2, is a safe method of preparing oxygen gas. Hydrogen peroxide decomposes slowly at room temperature but, in the presence of a catalyst (chemical that changes the rate of a reaction), decomposes more quickly. In this experiment, an enzyme (organic molecule that acts as a catalyst)—catalase—is used to increase the breakdown of hydrogen peroxide into water and oxygen molecules. The reaction is as follows:

$$2H_2O_2 \longrightarrow 2H_2O + O_2$$
hydrogen peroxide yields *water* plus *oxygen*

The test commonly used to identify oxygen gas is one by which a hot, glowing material bursts into flame when it is placed into a container of oxygen. Three requirements are necessary for burning to take place. The first is the presence of fuel (something that burns). The second is the presence of oxygen. The third is a **kindling temperature** (minimum temperature necessary for a substance to start burning). In this experiment, the wax is the fuel. Each bubble at the mouth of the jar is filled with oxygen. The glowing wick has enough energy to provide the kindling temperature, which is lower for pure oxygen than for air, since only about 21% of the air is oxygen.

Try New Approaches

1. Does temperature affect the speed of the oxygen-producing reaction? Repeat the experiment using three jars. Half fill each jar with hydrogen peroxide. Set one jar into each of the following water baths.

- Cold bath: Set the jar in a cup and surround it with ice.
- Moderate bath: Set the jar in a cup and fill the cup with cold tap water.
- Hot bath: Set the jar in a cup and fill the cup with hot tap water.

After five minutes, add equal amounts of meat to each jar and compare the speed of the oxygen bubbles produced. Are the bubbles larger in any of the jars?

2. Catalase is present in other kinds of living tissue, but do they contain the same amount? Repeat the original experiment two times, first using small pieces of potato, and then using small pieces of beef liver. Compare the amount and size of the bubbles produced by each food to determine the amount of enzyme present.

Design Your Own Experiment

1. Photosynthesis is an energy-producing reaction in which sugar, water, and oxygen are synthesized, in the presence of chlorophyll and light, from carbon dioxide and water. **Synthesis** is the forming of more complex molecules from simpler ones. For example, starch molecules are synthesized from simple molecules of sugar.

Plants are major contributors to atmospheric oxygen. Demonstrate the role of plants in producing oxygen and the fact that oxygen is a colorless, slightly soluble gas. Fill a large-mouthed jar three-fourths full with water. Place water plants such as elodea inside a funnel and set the funnel, mouth side down, in the jar of water. The stem of the funnel should be *above* the water level in the jar. Fill a small bottle (or test tube) with water. Place your thumb over the mouth of this bottle and invert it over the stem of the funnel. The mouth of the bottle must be *below* the water level in the jar (see Figure 26.2). Place the entire setup in a sunny area. Observe as bubbles of oxygen rise from the water plants and collect in the small bottle. Oxygen gas is not very soluble in water; thus, the gas displaces the water inside the bottle. When the bottle is full of oxygen, cap it and save the gas collected for the following experiment on rusting.

2. **Corrosion,** such as the rusting of iron, is the erosion and disintegration of a material. The rusting of an iron nail can be used to demonstrate the combination of iron atoms with oxygen atoms in the air to form iron oxide. The reaction for the rusting of iron is as follows:

$$4Fe \ + \ 3O_2 \ \longrightarrow \ 2Fe_2O_3$$
iron plus *oxygen* yields *iron oxide*

a. Does more oxygen speed up the oxidation (combination with oxygen) process? Use iron nails small enough to fit inside the bottle of oxygen gas previously collected. With steel wool, scrub the outside surface of two nails that have no rust on them. **CAUTION:** Use rubber gloves to protect your hands when handling the steel wool. Place one nail inside the bottle and secure the cap. Place the bottle and the second nail where they can remain undisturbed. Make daily observations of the nails for seven days.

b. Does iron rust faster when wet? Does acid rain increase the rate of rusting? Determine the effect of water and acids on the rusting of iron by using three equal-size pieces of steel wool. Wet one piece with water, wet a second piece by dipping it in vinegar, and leave the third piece dry. Place the steel wool pieces on separate saucers and allow them to sit exposed to the air for two days. Use a chemistry text to interpret the sequence of reactions produced by the observed results. You could use photographs to represent the daily changes. *Note:* You could extend this experiment by having relatives and/or friends who live in different cities collect rainwater. Then you could compare the rusting of the pieces of steel wool after they are dipped in the different rainwater samples.

3a. Other metals combine with oxygen, but the reaction with some metals, like copper, may take years. This slow oxidation rate can be observed by organizing a roll of pennies by their dates. The older coins are usually browner in color than the newer coins (unless they have been washed or kept in protective coverings). You can display sample

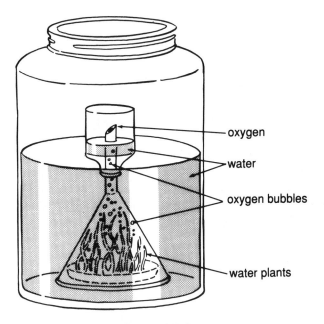

oxygen

water

oxygen bubbles

water plants

Figure 26.2

coins that show the change from a new shiny penny to an older brown-colored penny.

b. Does heat speed up the oxidation process? Choose two shiny pennies. Place one penny in an aluminum saucepan and heat for two minutes on the stove. Allow the penny to cool before removing. Compare the color of the heated penny with that of the unheated penny.

Get the Facts

1. Oxygen was discovered, but not recognized as a true element, by Carl Wilhelm Scheele in about 1772 and independently by Englishman Joseph Priestley in 1774. Antoine Lavoisier, a French chemist, extended and interpreted the experiments of Scheele and Priestley and gave the gas its name. Find out more about the discovery of oxygen. By what methods did Scheele and Priestley produce oxygen? What discoveries did Lavoisier make about the gas?

2. *LOX* (liquid oxygen) is used in many spacecraft for the very rapid combustion of the fuel needed to provide energy for liftoff. Find out more about the uses of oxygen such as the following:

- respiration
- treatment of water and sewage
- Manufacture of steel

- production of other chemical compounds (detergents, synthetic gasoline, antifreeze, alcohols)

3. Much is heard about the earth's ozone layer and its depletion. Use a chemistry text to find out more about this naturally occurring allotropic form of oxygen. An *allotrope* is the molecular form of an element that exists in two or more different forms, such as oxygen (O_2) and ozone (O_3). What are the physical and chemical differences between oxygen and ozone? How is oxygen converted into ozone? What is causing the damage to the ozone layer?

27 Carbon Dioxide: Its Production and Uses

Gases, like carbon dioxide, often cannot be seen, felt, or smelled. Yet gases are made of molecules and atoms that chemically react with other substances.

In this project, you will test for the presence of carbon dioxide. The physical and chemical properties of the gas will be examined. You will also look at means by which the gas is produced as well as some of its uses.

Getting Started

Purpose: To test for the presence of carbon dioxide when an acid and carbonate compound react.

Materials

glass soda bottle

¼ cup (63 ml) water

¼ cup of (63 ml) vinegar

scissors

ruler

tissue

1 teaspoon (5 ml) of baking soda

baby-food jar with lid

limewater (see Appendix 5)

modeling clay

flexible drinking straw

Procedure

1. Pour ¼ cup (63 ml) of water and ¼ cup (63 ml) vinegar into the bottle.

2. Cut a 3-inch (7.6-cm) strip of tissue.

3. Spread the baking soda across the center of the tissue.

4. Roll the paper around the baking soda. Secure the packet by twisting the ends of the paper.

5. Fill the baby-food jar three-fourths full with limewater.

6. Mold a walnut-size piece of clay around the end of the straw, on the end closest to the flexible section. (Do not cover the hole.)

7. Drop the packet of baking soda into the bottle.

8. Quickly plug the bottle's mouth with the clay around the straw. *Note:* The short end of the straw should be inside the bottle.

9. Hold the jar of limewater near the bottle so that the other end of the straw is beneath the surface of the limewater. (See Figure 27.1).

10. When the bubbling ceases, observe the limewater.

11. Secure the lid on the jar and allow the jar to stand undisturbed overnight.

12. Observe the contents of the jar.

Results

As bubbles from the straw enter the clear limewater, it turns milky. After standing, the solution looks clear, but there is a thin layer of white solid on the bottom of the jar.

Why?

Baking soda consists of the chemical compound sodium bicarbonate ($NaHCO_3$). Compounds containing carbonate (CO_3) react with acids such as vinegar (acetic acid) to produce carbon dioxide gas (CO_2). The equation for this reaction is as follows:

$$NaHCO_3 \quad + \quad HC_2H_3O_2 \longrightarrow$$
sodium   plus   *acetic*   yields
bicarbonate   *acid*

$$NaC_2H_3O_2 \quad + \quad H_2O \quad + \quad CO_2$$
sodium   plus *water* plus *carbon*
acetate   *dioxide*

    Limewater, $Ca(OH)_2$, is used to test for the presence of carbon dioxide gas because it reacts with carbon dioxide to form the compound calcium carbonate ($CaCO_3$). The equation for this reaction is as follows:

$$CO_2 \quad + \quad Ca(OH)_2 \longrightarrow CaCO_3(s) + \quad H_2O$$
carbon plus *calcium*   yields *calcium*   plus *water*
dioxide   *hydroxide*   *carbonate*

Note: The (s) in the equation indicates that calcium carbonate is insoluble. That is, it does not dissolve. The small white particles of insoluble calcium

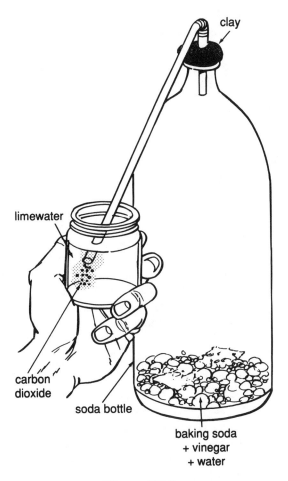

clay

limewater

carbon dioxide

soda bottle

baking soda
+ vinegar
+ water

Figure 27.1

carbonate temporarily stay suspended in the solution and give it a milky appearance. In time, gravity pulls the calcium carbonate to the bottom of the jar.

Try New Approaches

1. Does the use of a different acid alter the results? Repeat the experiment replacing the vinegar and water mixture with ½ cup (125 ml) of citric acid such as lemon juice or grapefruit juice.

2. Do other carbonated substances produce carbon dioxide when combined with acid? Repeat the original experiment replacing the baking soda with materials such as eggshells or marble chips, which contain calcium carbonate (limestone).

3. Carbon dioxide is a product of the fermentation of sugar. The reaction of the fermentation of sugar is as follows:

$$C_{12}H_{22}O_{11} \quad + \quad H_2O \quad + \quad yeast \quad \xrightarrow{\text{zymase}}$$
sucrose   plus *water* plus *yeast*   yields

$$4C_2H_5OH + \quad 4CO_2$$
ethyl   plus   *carbon*
alcohol   *dioxide*

Zymase is an enzyme (a chemical that changes the rate of a chemical reaction). Demonstrate the production of carbon dioxide by filling the soda bottle half full with water. Add 4 tablespoons (60 ml) of sucrose (table sugar) and ¼ ounce (7 g) of dry yeast. **Science Fair Hint:** Display photographs of the experiment along with the chemical equations of the reactions.

4. Drinking soda contains carbonated water, chemically known as carbonic acid (H_2CO_3). This acid readily decomposes to form water and carbon dioxide ($H_2CO_3 \longrightarrow H_2O + CO_2$). Limewater can be used to test for the presence of carbon dioxide in sodas. Repeat the original experiment replacing the empty soda bottle with a bottle filled with any brand of soda. Speed up the decomposition of the carbonated water by setting the soda bottle in a bowl of warm water. *Note:* Heat the soda bottle only if its cap has been removed.

Design Your Own Experiment

1. Organic fuels, which are compounds containing carbon (wax, for example), produce carbon dioxide when burned. Demonstrate this by burning a candle and collecting and testing the gas produced. Place about 1 inch (2.5 cm) of limewater in the bottom of a 1-quart (1-liter) jar. Wrap the end of a 12-inch (30-cm) wire around the center of a 2-inch (5-cm) long candle. Twist the wire to make a long handle (see Figure 27.2). Light the candle and hold the end of the wire to lower the candle into the jar. Cover part of the mouth of the jar with its lid.

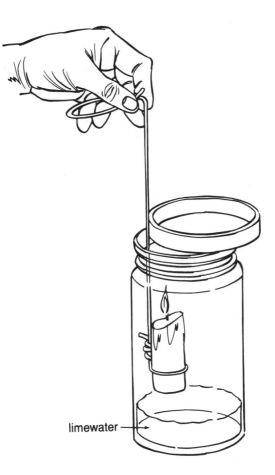

Figure 27.2

Allow the candle to burn until the flame goes out. Immediately remove the candle. Secure the lid on the jar and shake the jar vigorously four or five times. A milky solution indicates the presence of carbon dioxide. Display diagrams of a burning candle and of a car, indicating carbon dioxide molecules being emitted from the exhaust of the car and above the flame of the candle.

2. One of carbon dioxide's chemical properties is that it combines with limewater to produce insoluble calcium carbonate. Another important chemical property is that it does not burn or support combustion. Be-

cause of this property, carbon dioxide is used in fire extinguishers. Demonstrate this by wrapping a 12-inch (30-cm) wire around a 1-inch (2.5-cm) long candle. Light the candle and hold the end of the wire to lower the candle into a 1-quart (1-liter) jar. In a small-mouthed gallon jug mix together 1 teaspoon (5 ml) of baking soda, ¼ cup (63 ml) water, and ¼ cup (63 ml) of vinegar. When the fizzing stops, hold the mouth of the gallon jug over the mouth of the jar and slowly tilt the jug. Do not allow any liquid from the jug to enter the jar. The invisible, heavier-than-air carbon dioxide gas flows into the jar and extinguishes the flame. Display photographs showing the sequence of events in this reaction along with pictures of carbon dioxide fire extinguishers.

3. Respiration is the chemical process by which animals convert food into energy. Carbon dioxide is a by-product of this reaction and is expelled by the lungs. Test for this gas in your breath by exhaling through a straw into a soda bottle half filled with brom thymol blue solution (see Appendix 5). Brom thymol blue is an indicator that turns yellow in the presence of an acid. Carbon dioxide plus the water in the indicator produces carbonic acid resulting in a green to yellow color depending on the amount of carbon dioxide present.

Get the Facts

1. The temperature of the earth is kept warm due to gases, such as carbon dioxide, in the atmosphere. The atmospheric gases trap warmth from the sun, just as glass traps warmth in a greenhouse. For this reason, this warming of the earth is called the *greenhouse effect*. Scientist think the earth's atmosphere is getting warmer because of the increase of carbon dioxide production. Find out more about the greenhouse effect. The burning of fossil fuels is considered the major cause of the increase of carbon dioxide, but other factors contribute to the increase of this gas. What are they? If the earth's atmosphere is getting warmer, how much warmer is it? What effect does this extra heat have on the earth's environment? Can the warming be stopped?

2. Limestone caverns and the stalagmites and stalactites in these structures are formed from the combination of carbon dioxide and limewater in the soil. Find out more about the chemical reactions involved in the formation of limestone.

3. Find out more about the uses of carbon dioxide such as the following:

- carbonated drinks
- leavening agent in baking
- photosynthesis reaction
- stimulus for the nerve controlling the diaphragm

- agent in baking soda and washing soda made by the Solvay process
- solid carbon dioxide, dry ice, a refrigerant

28 Thermodynamics: Energy Transfer

Your daily life brings you in contact with hot and cold objects. You observe that iced drinks get warmer and hot drinks get cooler. These everyday experiences can be explained by thermodynamics, the study of energy movement. Thermodynamics is from the Greek word *thermos,* which means "heat," and dynamics, which implies movement.

In this project, you will determine the direction of energy transfer of two materials. Calculations of heat content will be made. You will study the effect that a substance's specific heat has on the amount of energy needed to change the temperature of the substance, and you will also determine the specific heat of a substance.

Getting Started

Purpose: To determine the direction of energy transfer when two materials of different temperatures are placed together.

Materials

2-quart (2-liter) metal teakettle with lid	ruler
water	scissors
stove	string
1-quart (1-liter) bowl	3 stainless steel nails (16-penny size)
thermometer	tongs

Procedure

1. Fill the teakettle three-fourths full with water and heat it.
2. While waiting for the water to boil, fill the bowl half full with cold tap water.
3. Use the thermometer to measure the temperature of the cold water in the bowl. Record this temperature as the initial temperature of the water.
4. Measure and cut a 12-inch (30-cm) piece of string.

5. Tie the nails together with one end of the string.

6. Lower the nails into the kettle of boiling water so that the nails are positioned in the center of the water.

7. Lay the string over the top of the kettle and close the lid. *Note:* The lid should hold the string stationary with the nails suspended in the water (see Figure 28.1).

8. Heat the nails for five minutes. The metal in the nails will heat to the temperature of the boiling water, which is 212°F (100°C). Record this temperature as the initial temperature of the metal.

9. Use tongs to move the nails from the boiling water.

10. Shake off as much of the hot water as possible from the nails and immediately immerse the nails into the bowl of cold water.

11. Gently stir the water with the thermometer (see Figure 28.2).

12. Observe the temperature of the water in the bowl. When the water reaches a constant temperature, stop stirring and record this temperature as the final temperature for both the metal and the water.

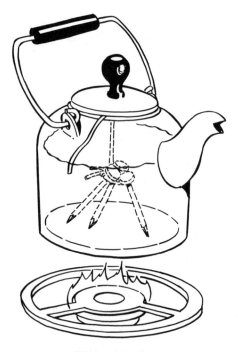

Figure 28.1

13. Calculate the change in temperature of the metal and the water by taking the absolute difference (subtracting the smaller from the larger number) between the initial and final temperatures of each. See Appendix 1 for an example calculation.

14. Construct a data table such as the one shown here.

Data Table		
Temperature	Metal	Water
initial		
final		
change		

Results

The exact change of temperature of the water and the metal depends on the amount and initial temperature of the water in the bowl. Other factors

Figure 28.2

affecting the temperature changes of materials will be studied later, but, in this experiment, the metal makes the greater temperature change.

Why?

According to **thermodynamics** (the study of energy movement), when two materials at different temperatures are placed together, such as the hot nails and the cold water, heat is transferred from the hotter to the colder material. This exchange of heat continues until both materials finally reach the same temperature. If you assume that no heat is lost to the surrounding area, then the heat gained by the water is lost by the nails. The mixture is an example of the first law of thermodynamics, which states that the total energy of the isolated system is constant. The energy remains constant because as the energy of one part of the mixture increases, the energy of another part decreases.

Try New Approaches

1. Does the type of metal affect the results? Repeat the experiment replacing the iron nails with nails of equal size but that are galvanized or made from other metals such as aluminum.
2. Does the quantity of the substances affect the temperature change?
   a. Repeat the original experiment two times, first decreasing the amount of cold water in the bowl by half, and then using twice as much water.
   b. Repeat the original experiment two more times, first using one nail, and then using nine nails.

Science Fair Hint: Display photographs with temperature labels to represent the procedure and results.

Design Your Own Experiment

1. The reason for the difference in the change of temperature of the water and the metals is due to their specific heats (energy required to raise the temperature of one gram of matter one degree Celsius). The value of the specific heat varies for each substance, and water has one of the highest specific heats. Thus, more heat has to be gained or lost to change the temperature of water.
   Demonstrate this by filling three Styrofoam® cups each three-

fourths full, one with water, one with sodium chloride (table salt), and one with sucrose (table sugar). Allow the cups to stand at room temperature until the temperatures of the contents of the cups are equal. Place the cups in a freezer for two hours. Remove them from the freezer and insert a thermometer in each. Record the temperature immediately and every 15 minutes until one of the materials reaches room temperature.

2. Land and sea breezes are caused by the difference in the specific heats of water and soil. During the day, the land heats more quickly than the sea. Hot air above the land rises, and cooler air above the sea rushes in to take the place of the rising warm air. This air movement produces a sea breeze. At night, the land cools faster than the sea. The hotter air above the sea rises, and the cooler air above the land rushes toward the sea to create a land breeze.

Demonstrate this by filling two Styrofoam® cups half full, one with water and the other with soil. Place a thermometer in each cup and set the cups together on a table until their temperatures are equal. Position a desk lamp so that the light evenly hits both cups (see Figure 28.3). Record the temperature on each thermometer after two hours. Turn the light off and record the temperature on each thermometer every 15 minutes for one hour. Display photographs of this experiment along with diagrams showing the movement of air during sea and land breezes.

3. The heat of materials can be calculated with the following equation:

heat (Q) = mass × specific heat × temperature change

The specific heat value for water is one calorie per one gram per one degree Celsius. Thus, it takes one calorie of heat to change one gram of water one degree Celsius. With the specific heat of water and the fact that in a mixture the heat lost equals the heat gained, Q (gained) = Q (lost), the specific heat of a substance can be calculated.

Demonstrate by cooling or heating a substance with water. Weigh 50 ml of corn syrup and pour it into a Styrofoam cup. Place the cup of syrup in a freezer for one hour and then determine its temperature. Pour 50 ml of hot tap water into a measuring cup and determine its temperature. Add the hot water to the cold syrup. Stir. Then cover with a second Styrofoam cup. Tape the cups together and insert a thermometer through a hole in the top cup. Stir the solution with the ther-

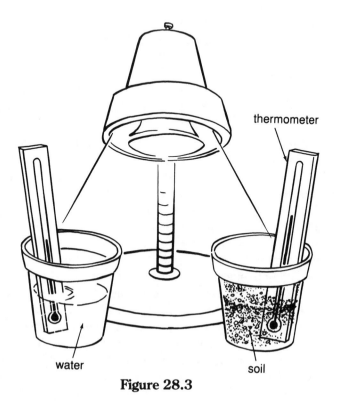

Figure 28.3

mometer until the temperature remains constant. Record the final temperature. Calculate the specific heat of the syrup, assuming the Styrofoam cup does not change temperature. See Appendix 12 for an example calculation.

Get the Facts

1. The heat required to raise the temperature of a substance varies depending on its *phase* (solid, liquid, or gas). Use a chemistry text to find out more about specific heats. You could display a chart comparing the values of common materials.

2. Heat is not always where you want it or when you want it. Solar heating is a prime example. The windows on the south side of a solar home receive more direct sunlight than those on the other sides, and the sun does not shine at night. Solar homes need a way to store solar energy. Find out more about materials used for heat storage. What materials make good "heat sponges" for absorbing heat during the day but cooling down slowly at night? What are the advantages and disadvantages of some of the materials used to store heat?

29 | Thermometers: Old and New

Temperature is how hot or cold something is as indicated by a particular scale of measurement. Your body is sensitive to degrees of hotness or coldness of an object but not to specific temperatures. From as early as 1593, thermometers have been used to measure temperature.

In this project, you will study the progression of measuring temperature from the earliest open-air thermometer designed by the Italian physicist Galileo Galilei called a "thermoscope" to modern thermometers that use "chameleon" chemicals to indicate temperature. You will also look at the algebraic relationships between the Fahrenheit, Celsius, and Kelvin temperature scales.

Getting Started

Purpose: To construct a model of Galileo's gas thermometer.

Materials

water

1-quart (1-liter) jar

blue food coloring

drinking straw

glass soda bottle

modeling clay

Procedure

1. Pour about 2 inches (5 cm) of water into the jar.

2. Add drops of blue food coloring to make the water in the jar a deep blue.

3. Insert about 2 inches (5 cm) of the end of the straw into the mouth of the soda bottle.

4. Mold a piece of clay around the straw and seal the mouth of the bottle.

5. Wrap your hands around the sides of the bottle. Press as much of the palms of your hands as possible against the glass, but do not press hard enough to break the glass.

6. Hold the bottle in your hands for one minute (see Figure 29.1).

7. Stand the bottle, straw down, in the jar of colored water so that the straw extends below the surface of the water (see Figure 29.2).

8. Observe the straw for two to three minutes.

Results

The colored water rises in the straw.

Why?

A **thermometer** is used to measure the average energy of motion of molecules. The bottle is a simplified model of Galileo's gas thermometer. Galileo designed his thermometer, which he called a "thermoscope," in 1593. The thermoscope and the bottle thermometer both make use of the fact that gas expands when heated and contracts when cooled to indicate a

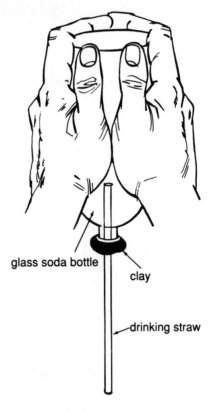

glass soda bottle

clay

drinking straw

Figure 29.1

change in temperature. The bottle and straw are filled with air. Holding the bottle in your hands causes the gas inside to be heated. The heated gas molecules **expand** (move faster and farther apart) and escape through the end of the straw. As the bottle cools, the gas molecules that are left in the bottle **contract** (move slower and closer together). Since there are now fewer molecules in the bottle, they take up less space and a partial **vacuum** (an empty space) is created. The pressure inside the bottle is less than the atmospheric pressure outside; thus, air pushing on the surface of the water forces water into the straw.

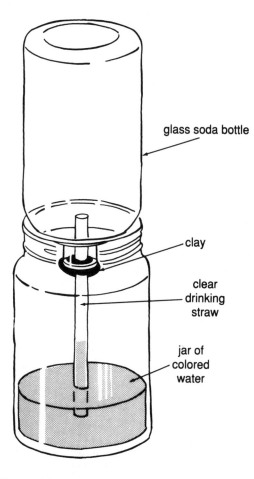

glass soda bottle

clay

clear drinking straw

jar of colored water

Figure 29.2 Model of Galileo's Thermometer

Try New Approaches

1. Does adding more energy affect the results? Repeat the experiment standing the bottle in a bowl containing 2 inches (5 cm) of hot tap water. Mark the height of the water column in the straw or its level in the bottle. Use a thermometer to measure the temperature in degrees Fahrenheit or Celsius.

2. Do thermometers measure the temperature or heat content of a substance? Temperature is the measure of the kinetic energy (energy of motion) of the molecules, and heat is the combined energy of all the molecules in the substance. Demonstrate the difference between the temperature and heat content by filling a large baking pan with 2 inches (5 cm) of warm water at the same temperature as that used in the previous experiment. Set the bottle thermometer in the bowl of water and observe the height of the water column in the straw or inside the bottle. *Note:* It is important to use the same height of water so that the same number of gas molecules inside the bottle are heated. **Science Fair Hint:** Display photographs of the thermoscope model.

3. Does cooling the bottle affect the results? Repeat the original experiment setting the bottle in a bowl of ice water. **Science Fair Hint:** Display diagrams of the thermoscope model showing the movement of air in and out of the straw as the bottle is heated and cooled.

Design Your Own Experiment

1. Make another gas thermometer by standing a straw with a 7/32-inch (0.56-cm) diameter in a cup half filled with water tinted with food coloring. While the straw is in the water, place your index finger over the open end of the straw. Hold the straw closed with your finger while lifting the straw out of the colored water and inserting the free end into an empty soda bottle. Seal the mouth of the bottle by wrapping clay around the straw. Observe how the colored plug of water rises and lowers in the straw as the air in the bottle is heated and cooled.

2. In 1623, a French physician, Jean Rey, designed a liquid thermometer. This instrument worked because liquids, like gases, expand and contract when heated. Construct a model of the Rey thermometer by filling a glass soda bottle with water tinted with food coloring. Insert about 2 inches (5 cm) of the end of a drinking straw into the bottle

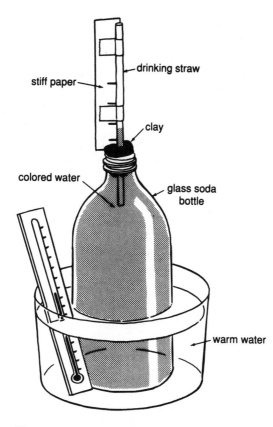

stiff paper

drinking straw

clay

colored water

glass soda
bottle

warm water

Figure 29.3   Model of Rey's Thermometer
with a Fixed Scale

of colored water. Seal the mouth of the bottle by wrapping clay
around the straw. Stand the bottle in a bowl of warm water.

3a. Galileo's and Rey's thermometers had no fixed scale. The first thermometer scale was suggested by Christian Huygens (1629–1695), a
Dutch mathematician, astronomer, and physicist. He used only one
fixed point (either the freezing or the boiling point of water). In 1714,
Gabriel Fahrenheit, a German scientist, introduced a simple mercury
thermometer with a scale. Add a scale to your Rey thermometer
model by attaching a piece of stiff paper to the straw with tape. Measure the temperature of the water in order to mark the Rey scale.
(See Figure 29.3.) Try different straw and/or tube sizes.

b. What effect does atmospheric pressure have on the accuracy of open thermometers? Repeat the original experiment using the Rey thermometer with its scale and/or add a scale to the Galileo thermometer. Measure the atmospheric pressure with a barometer or secure the information from a television or radio weather forecast. Take measurements on different days with varying atmospheric pressures. Display a chart of the results.

4. Draw diagrams comparing the Fahrenheit, Celsius, and Kelvin thermometer scales. Use the following algebraic equations to compute temperatures for each of the three scales. See Appendix 13 for example calculations.

   a. Relationship between Fahrenheit and Celsius:

   Celsius to Fahrenheit
   $$°F = (1.8 \times °C) + 32$$

   Fahrenheit to Celsius
   $$°C = \frac{°F - 32}{1.8}$$

   b. Relationship between Celsius and Kelvin

   Celsius to Kelvin
   $$K = °C + 273$$

   Kelvin to Celsius
   $$°C = K - 273$$

   Display the diagrams and a few computations. Indicate common and interesting temperatures such as the average person's body temperature of 98.6°F, the boiling point of water at 100°C, and the freezing point of water at 273 K.

Get the Facts

The Italian physicist Galileo's thermoscope is the first known instrument used to measure temperature. Find out more about the development and uses of thermometers. What did the thermoscope look like? How was the

Florentine thermometer different from the Rey liquid thermometer? Who introduced the first mercury thermometer? What was used to determine the first thermometer scales? Include information about the thermometer introduced by Gabriel D. Fahrenheit, Anders Celsius, and Lord Kelvin. Find out about the use of digital thermometers and heat-sensitive "chameleon" chemicals that change colors.

30 Insulators: Resistors to Heat Flow

The process of heating and cooling a building is expensive and requires a great deal of energy. The expense plus the need to save energy have focused the attention of scientists on studying how to restrict heat flow by using insulating materials.

In this project, you will compare the insulating ability of different materials. The conductivity of materials and the reflective nature of solar energy will be determined. You will also look at the methods of energy transfer.

Getting Started

Purpose: To determine whether sand has insulating properties.

Materials

cardboard box at least 2 inches (5 cm) taller and wider than one of the jars

sand

2 1-quart (1-liter) jars with lids

1-cup (250 ml) measuring cup

water

2 thermometers

Procedure

1. Cover the bottom of the box with 1 inch (2.5 cm) of sand.
2. Set one jar in the box.
3. Fill the box with sand up to the top of the jar.
4. Use the measuring cup to add 2 cups (500 ml) of hot water to each jar.
5. Stand one thermometer in each jar of hot tap water for one minute (see Figure 30.1).
6. Read and record the temperature of the water in each jar.
7. Remove the thermometer and seal the jars with their lids.
8. Quickly cover the jar in the box with a 1-inch (2.5-cm) layer of sand.

189

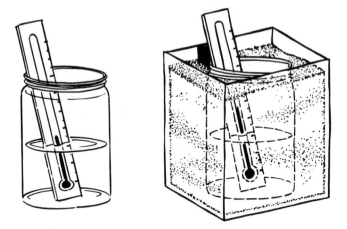

Figure 30.1

9. Close the lid on the box.

10. Allow the jars to remain undisturbed for ten minutes.

11. Uncover the jars and stand one thermometer in each jar.

12. Allow the thermometers to stand for one minute.

13. Read and record the temperature of the water in each jar.

Results

The water in the jar that is placed in the box surrounded by sand stays warmer longer than the water in the uncovered jar does.

Why?

Heat energy moves from a warm area to a cooler area. The water inside the jars is warmer than the sand and the air outside the jars. As heat flows from the warm water to the materials outside the jars, water in the jars cools. The water in the jar that is placed in the box surrounded by sand stays warmer longer because the heat is slowly conducted out of the water into the sand. The heat leaves the water in the uncovered jar more quickly as it flows to the cooler air outside.

The rate of heat flow from a material depends on what surrounds it. An **insulator** is something that restricts or retards heat flow. A good insulator, such as the sand, slows the energy flow. Thus, the water surrounded by sand is kept warmer for a longer period of time.

Try New Approaches

1. Compare the insulating properties of other materials. Repeat the experiment replacing the sand with other materials such as cotton balls, feathers, polystyrene beads, and crumpled balls of paper. Loosely pack the materials in the box. **Science Fair Hint:** Display samples of the testing materials in order from the one with the greatest to the one with the least insulating property.

2. A vacuum is the best insulation, but next best is motionless air. Do the insulating properties of the previously used materials depend on the amount of trapped pockets of dead air they have? Repeat the previous experiment tightly packing each material in the box to squeeze out as much air as possible.

Design Your Own Experiment

1a. How much heat energy is lost through windows? Use three 1-quart (1-liter) jars with lids. Fill the jars half full with hot tap water and secure the lids. Set one jar in a box and fill the box with sand up to the lid of the jar. Leave enough space to remove the jar's lid easily. Place the second jar in a box with sand covering half of the jar. Stand the third jar in a box and do not use any sand to cover it. Remove the jars' lids and measure the temperature of the water in the containers. Again, secure the lids on the jars. Again remove the jars' lids and measure the temperature of the water in the containers once every five minutes until the water in the jars reaches the same temperature. Be sure to replace the lid quickly after each temperature reading. You could display a graph of the temperature readings.

b. Many windows in buildings and cars are covered with a solar film. What effect does the covering have on controlling the temperature inside a building or car? Repeat the previous experiment replacing the sand insulation with solar film. Check (under glass coating and tinting materials) in your telephone directory for companies that carry solar film.

2. Heat reaches the earth by means of radiation. This heat can be reflected. Demonstrate the reflection of radiated heat by replacing two thermometers in a shaded area. Hold a mirror so that the sun's light is reflected onto the bulb of one of the thermometers. Ask a helper to observe the temperature readings on both thermometers.

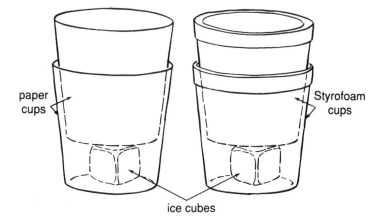

paper
cups

Styrofoam
cups

ice cubes

Figure 30.2

CAUTION: Stop the experiment after one minute or if one thermometer reading nears the highest measurement on the scale.

3a. Another method of comparing the insulating properties of materials is to observe the rate at which an ice cube melts. Put an ice cube inside a paper cup. Slip a second paper cup inside the first one so that it rests on top of the ice cube. Put an ice cube inside a Styrofoam® cup and, as before, slip a second Styrofoam cup inside the first one (see Figure 30.2). Lift the top cups and observe the ice cubes once every five minutes. Continue until one of the ice cubes completely melts. You could graph and display the results.

b. Are thicker cups better insulators? Repeat the previous experiment using a different number of cups. Try four cups with an ice cube between them.

4. Some materials conduct or transfer heat better than others. Place the bowls of a wooden, a plastic, and a metal spoon in a 1-pint (500-ml) jar. Use equal-size balls of margarine to secure plastic beads to the handles of the spoons, with all the beads at the same height from the bottom of the jar. Pour about 4 inches (10 cm) of hot water into the jar (see Figure 30.3). As heat is conducted up a spoon, the margarine melts, causing the bead to fall. The faster the bead falls, the faster the heat energy is conducted up the spoon. Rate the conductivity of the materials. You could display the results along with photographs taken during the experiment.

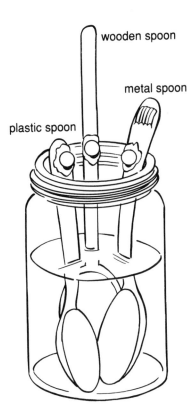

wooden spoon

metal spoon

plastic spoon

Figure 30.3

Get the Facts

1. The surface of NASA's space shuttle is covered with special insulating tiles. Obtain information about these special tiles, which help control the temperature inside the spacecraft. Write to NASA, Lyndon B. Johnson Center, Mail Code AP-4, 2101 NASA Road #1, Houston, TX 77058.

2. Heat energy is transferred from one place to another by conduction, convection, and radiation. Find out more about these three methods of energy transportation. Use the facts about energy movement to explain how insulation helps to keep a house cooler in the summer and warmer in the winter.

APPENDIX 1

Absolute Difference

The absolute difference between any two numbers is always a positive number. To achieve it, always subtract the smaller value from the larger value.

To find the change in temperature, calculate the absolute difference between the two temperature values.

Example:

$$\text{initial temperature} = 56°F$$

$$\text{final temperature} = 126°F$$

$$\text{temperature change} = \text{final temperature} - \text{initial temperature}$$
$$= 126°F - 56°F$$
$$= \mathbf{70°F}$$

Food Calories

Calculate the amount of food Calories released if the heat from a burning peanut changes the temperature of 50 g of water from 23°C to 25°C.

a. Calculate the gram calories released:

$$\begin{aligned}
\text{gram calories} &= \text{mass of water} \times \text{temperature change} \\
&\quad \times \text{specific heat} \\
&= 50 \text{ g} \times 2°C \times 1 \text{ cal/g·°C} \\
&= 100 \text{ g·°C} \times 1 \text{ cal/g·°C} \\
&= \textbf{100 cal}
\end{aligned}$$

b. Convert gram calories to food Calories:

$$\begin{aligned}
\text{food Calories} &= \frac{\text{gram calories}}{1{,}000} \\
&= \frac{100 \text{ gram calories}}{1{,}000} \\
&= \textbf{0.1 food Calorie}
\end{aligned}$$

APPENDIX 3

Calorie Counter

On the average, a 150-pound (68-kg) person will burn the following number of calories per hour (cph) while involved in the indicated activity.

Activity	cph
Driving a car	120
Gardening	220
Sitting (watching TV, reading, writing)	100
Sleeping or lying down	80
Sports	
Bicycling (5.5 mph)	210
Bicycling (10 mph)	900
Bowling	270
Cross-country skiing (10 mph)	600
Dancing	350
Golfing	250
Roller skating	350
Running (10 mph)	900
Squash	600
Swimming (¼ mile)	300
Tennis	420
Standing	140
Walking fast	300
Walking slowly	210
Domestic work (cleaning your room, washing dishes, sweeping)	180

Energy Input and Output

The following information is for a person weighing 150 pounds (68 kg). All reference to the person will be made as "the test subject." Energy input and output are determined for a 24-hour test period.

Energy Input

Energy input is equal to the number of food Calories in the food eaten. Use a calorie counter chart found in a nutrition text to determine the food Calories eaten by the test subject in a 24-hour test period. The number of Calories in the food eaten by the test subject was determined to be as follows:

Energy input = **5,000 Calories**

Calorie Expenditure Chart for the Test Subject

Activity	Time Spent (hours)	× cph (cph found in Appendix 3)	= Calories Expended
Bicycling	0.5	210	105
Sleeping	8	80	640
Sitting (watching TV, working at a computer, reading)	11.5	100	1,150
Walking (2.5 mph)	2	210	420
Total Calories Expended			2,315

Specific Dynamic Action (SDA) for Test Subject

SDA = 10% of energy input (Calories eaten)
= 10% × 5,000 Calories
= **500 Calories**

Basal Metabolism for Test Subject

$$\text{basal metabolism} = \text{test period} \times \text{body weight} \times \frac{1 \text{ Calorie}}{\text{hr} \cdot \text{kg}}$$

(Calories)   (hours)   (kilograms)

$$= 24 \text{ hours} \times 68 \text{ kg} \times \frac{1 \text{ Calorie}}{\text{hr} \cdot \text{kg}}$$

$$= 1,632 \text{ Calories}$$

Energy Stored

Energy stored is calculated as follows:

$$\text{energy stored} = \text{energy input} - \text{energy output}$$

A positive (+) energy stored calculation indicates a gain of body fat, and thus a gain in body weight. A negative stored energy indicates that energy calories were taken from body fat resulting in a loss of weight.

$$\text{energy stored} = 5,000 \text{ C} - (2,315 \text{ C} + 500\text{C} + 1,632 \text{ C})$$

$$= + 553 \text{ Calories}$$

Preparing Testing Solutions

Brom Thymol Blue

Materials

1-quart (1-liter) jar with lid

1 quart (1 liter) of distilled water

0.1 gram of brom thymol blue

Procedure

1. Fill the jar with distilled water.
2. Add the brom thymol blue to the jar.
3. Secure the lid and shake the jar to mix. *Note:* If the solution appears green or yellow, add one drop of household ammonia (one drop at a time) until the indicator appears blue.

Calcium Hydroxide (Limewater)

Materials

2 1-quart (1-liter) glass jars with lids

distilled water

calcium oxide (lime used to make pickles)

masking tape

marking pen

Procedure

1. Fill one jar with distilled water.
2. Add 1 teaspoon (5 ml) of calcium oxide and stir.
3. Secure the lid and allow the solution to stand overnight.
4. Decant (pour off) the clear liquid into the second jar. Be careful not to pour any of the lime that has settled on the bottom of the jar.
5. Secure the lid and keep the jar closed.

6. Use masking tape and a marking pen to label the jar "Limewater."

Monosaccharide Testing Solution

Materials

copper scrubbing pad

½-pint (250-ml) jar with lid

household ammonia

piece of cardboard large enough to cover top of jar

Procedure

1. Put the scrubbing pad into the jar.

2. Fill the jar with the ammonia.

3. Cover the top of the jar with the cardboard to reduce the escaping ammonia smell.

4. Place the covered jar where it can remain undisturbed for 24 hours.

5. Remove the scrubbing pad.

6. Secure the lid on the jar and store in a cool area.

Phenolphthalein

Materials

4 tablespoons (60 ml) of rubbing alcohol

2 baby-food jars (one with a lid)

1 Ex-Lax® tablet

spoon

Procedure

1. Pour the rubbing alcohol into the first jar.

2. Break the Ex-Lax tablet into small pieces and place them in the jar of alcohol.

3. Use the spoon to crush and stir the tablet pieces. *Note:* The tablet will not dissolve completely. Pieces will settle to the bottom of the solution.

4. Decant the clearer liquid at the top into a clean jar.

5. Secure the lid on the jar to store.

Red Cabbage Extract

Materials

small head of red cabbage   tea strainer
2-quart (2-liter) cooking pot   1-quart (1-liter) jar with lid
distilled water

Procedure

CAUTION: Take care when heating the liquid and do not remove the pot from the stove until it cools to room temperature.

1. Tear or cut the cabbage leaves into small pieces and place them in the cooking pot.
2. Fill the pot with distilled water.
3. Boil for five minutes. Allow to cool to room temperature.
4. Pour the cooled cabbage extract through the tea strainer into the jar. Discard the cabbage leaves.
5. Store the concentrated cabbage extract in a refrigerator until needed.
6. When ready to use, mix equal parts of the concentrated cabbage extract and distilled water.

Sodium Chloride Solution (0.9%)

Materials

9 grams of sodium chloride   1-quart (1-liter) jar
  (table salt)
991 ml of distilled water

Procedure

1. Combine the sodium chloride and water in the jar.
2. Stir until the sodium chloride dissolves.

Note: The following procedure is a little less accurate, but it is fine for most experiments in this book.

1. Combine 1 teaspoon of sodium chloride with 1 quart (1 liter) of distilled water.
2. Stir until the sodium chloride dissolves.

Starch Solution (1%)

Materials

½ teaspoon (2.5 ml) of cornstarch

1 cup (250 ml) of distilled water

small saucepan

1-pint (500-ml) jar with lid

Procedure

1. Mix the starch with 1 tablespoon (15 ml) of the water to form a paste.
2. Boil the remaining water in the saucepan and slowly add the starch paste.
3. Cook for two minutes, stirring constantly. Allow to cool.
4. Pour into the jar and secure the lid.

Vitamin C Content in Food

If it takes 50 drops of iodine to react with 25 mg of vitamin C, determine the number of milligrams of vitamin C in a fruit juice if 20 drops of iodine reacted with the juice.

$$\frac{? \text{ mg of vit. C in juice}}{20 \text{ drops of iodine}} = \frac{25 \text{ mg of vit. C}}{50 \text{ drops of iodine}}$$

$$? \text{ mg of vit. C in juice} = \frac{25 \text{ mg of vit. C} \times 20 \text{ drops of iodine}}{50 \text{ drops of iodine}}$$

$$= \textbf{10 mg of vit. C}$$

Normality

Normality (N) is a concentration unit used to measure the number of **equivalents** (quantities of substances that have the same combining capacity) per liter of solution. The number of equivalents of an acid or a base can be calculated by multiplying the normality of a solution times its volume in liters. Adding a measured amount of a base to a measured amount of an acid is a laboratory process called *titration*. During titration, the acids and bases chemically react in equivalent amounts. *Note:* As long as both the acid and base have the same volume unit any measuring unit may be used including drops.

Example:

In a titration, 30.0 ml of 0.04 N ammonium hydroxide is added to 20.0 ml of hydrochloric acid. What is the normality of the hydrochloric acid? *Note:* Since the units of both volume measurements are milliliters, there is no need to change them to liters. Also, the equation that follows uses the symbols N for normality and V for volume.

$$N \text{ (acid)} \times V \text{ (acid)} = N \text{ (base)} \times V \text{ (base)}$$
$$N \text{ (acid)} \times 20.0 \text{ ml} = 0.04 \text{ N} \times 30.0 \text{ ml}$$
$$N \text{ (acid)} = \frac{0.04 \text{ N} \times 30.0 \text{ ml}}{20.0 \text{ ml}}$$
$$= \textbf{0.06 N}$$

APPENDIX 8
Calibration of an Eyedropper

To measure the amount of liquid added with an eyedropper, first determine the volume of one drop. Do this by filling the eyedropper with water and counting the drops needed to fill 1 teaspoon (5 ml). Divide the number of drops by 5 ml to calculate the number of milliliters per drop from the eyedropper. It took 97 drops from the author's eyedropper to fill 1 teaspoon (5 ml); thus, each drop from the eyedropper has a volume of 19.4 ml (97 drops divided by 5 ml).

APPENDIX 9

Flow Rate (R)

Every food dye has a unique molecular structure that causes a difference in solubility and adhesion or affinity for the chromatographic paper. As a result, each dye is carried to different heights by the rising solvent. The distance each dye travels is measured from the start line on the paper to the center of the color band formed (see Figure A.1). The average distance traveled by the color solute and the solvent is known as the flow rate (R) and is calculated by using the following formula:

$$R = \frac{D_1 \text{ (distance the solute travels)}}{D_2 \text{ (distance the solvent travels)}}$$

Example:
A solvent travels 10 cm, and the distance from the start line to the center of the color band is 4.8 cm. Calculate the flow rate for the color band in question.

$$R = \frac{4.8 \text{ cm}}{10 \text{ cm}} = 0.48$$

Note: Only metric units are shown because it is easier to measure small distances with this system.

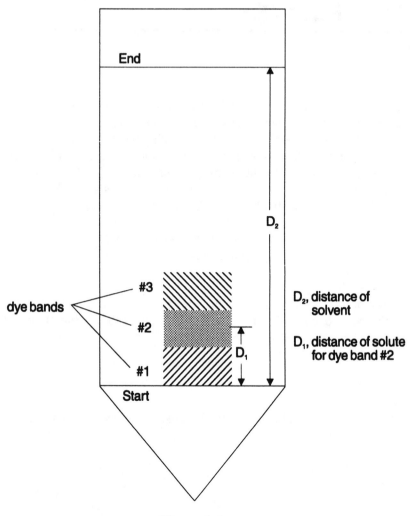

Figure A.1

APPENDIX 10

Viscosity Index

Viscosity measures how the thickness of a liquid resists its ability to flow. Viscosity index is a comparison of the flow rate of a liquid to that of water. Calculate the viscosity index of a dishwashing liquid using the following facts:

- flow rate of the dishwashing liquid = 573 seconds
- flow rate of water = 39.3 seconds

$$\text{viscosity index} = \frac{\text{flow rate of liquid}}{\text{flow rate of water}}$$
$$= \frac{573 \text{ seconds}}{39.3 \text{ seconds}}$$
$$= \mathbf{14.58}$$

This number indicates that the dishwashing liquid is 14.58 times as viscous as is water.

APPENDIX 11

Density

Density of a Box

Example:
A box measuring 4 cm × 6 cm × 8 cm has a mass of 768 grams. Determine the density of the box using the following facts:

- density = mass/volume
- mass = 768 grams
- volume = length × width × height
  = 4 cm × 6 cm × 8 cm
  = 192 cubic centimeters

> density = 768 grams/192 cubic centimeters
> = **4 grams/cubic centimeter**

Density of a Sphere

Example:
A sphere with a circumference of 15 cm has a mass of 229 grams. Determine the density of the sphere using the following facts:

- density of a sphere = mass/volume
- mass = 229 grams
- volume of a sphere = ⅘ × pi (3.14) × radius cubed
- Since the radius is not given, it will have to be calculated using the circumference of the sphere. That is,

> circumference = 2 × pi (3.14) × radius

Thus,

$$\text{radius} = \frac{\text{circumference}}{2 \times 3.14}$$
$$= \frac{15 \text{ cm}}{2 \times 3.14}$$
$$= 2.39 \text{ cm}$$

$$\text{density} = \frac{229 \text{ g}}{\frac{4}{3} \times 3.14 \times (2.39 \text{ cm})^3}$$

$$= 4 \text{ g/cm}^3$$

APPENDIX 12

Heat Content (Q)

The heat content of a substance can be calculated by using the following equation:

$$\text{heat (Q)} = \text{mass (m)} \times \text{specific heat (C)}$$
$$\times \text{temperature change (T)}$$
$$Q = m \times C \times T$$

When two materials having different temperatures are mixed together, the hotter material loses energy and the cooler material gains energy. The total amount of energy gained equals the total amount of energy lost. This first law of thermodynamics can be expressed by the following equation:

$$Q \text{ (lost)} = Q \text{ (gained)}$$

Example: A 30-gram piece of metal at 90°C is placed in 50 ml (50 grams) of water at 25°C. After a short time, the temperature of both metal and water is 35°C. On the basis of these measurements and the fact that the specific heat (energy required to raise the temperature of one gram matter one degree Celsius) for water is 1 cal/g·°C, what is the specific heat of the metal?

$$Q \text{ (metal)} = Q \text{ (water)}$$

$$m \times C \times T = m \times C \times T$$

$$30 \text{ g} \times C \times (90°C - 35°C) = 50 \text{ g} \times 1 \text{ cal/g·°C} \times (35°C - 25°C)$$
$$30 \text{ g} \times C \times 55°C = 50 \text{ g} \times 1 \text{ cal/g·°C} \times 10°C$$

$$C = \frac{50 \text{ g} \times 1 \text{ cal/g·°C} \times 10°C}{30 \text{ g} \times 55°C}$$
$$= \frac{500 \text{ g·°C} \times 1 \text{ cal/g·°C}}{1,650 \text{ g·°C}}$$
$$= 0.303 \times 1 \text{ cal/g·°C}$$

$$C \text{ (metal)} = \textbf{0.303 cal/g·°C}$$

Temperature Scales

Celsius to Fahrenheit

Example: Change 100 degrees Celsius to Fahrenheit.

$$F = (1.8) \times °C + 32$$
$$= (1.8) \times 100 + 32$$
$$= 180 + 32$$
$$= \textbf{212°F}$$

Fahrenheit to Celsius

Example: Change 212 degrees Fahrenheit to Celsius.

$$°C = \frac{°F - 32}{1.8}$$
$$= \frac{212 - 32}{1.8}$$
$$= \textbf{100°C}$$

Celsius to Kelvin

Example: Change 30 degrees Celsius to Kelvin.

$$K = °C + 273$$
$$= 30 + 273$$
$$= \textbf{303 K}$$

Kelvin to Celsius

Example: Change 303 degrees Kelvin to Celsius.

$$°C = K - 273$$
$$= 303 - 273$$
$$= \textbf{30°C}$$

Glossary

absolute difference   An absolute value is a positive number; thus, an absolute difference is calculated by subtracting a smaller number from a larger number.

acid   Compound containing hydrogen ions.

adhesion   Force of attraction between unlike molecules.

adsorption   The adhesion of any kind of atom molecule or ion to the surface of solid bodies with which they come in contact.

amines   Organic chemicals associated with decaying flesh; an organic base containing an amino group.

anhydrous   Chemical form of a substance existing without being combined with water of crystallization.

anion   Negative chemical particles.

anode   Conductor connected to, or the positive terminal of, a battery.

atmospheric pressure   Pressure of the weight of the atmospheric gases that push against the earth.

basal metabolism   All the work that goes on inside the human body to keep it alive.

base   Chemical containing hydroxide ions.

biochemistry   Chemical reactions in living organisms.

blanching   Process of cooking vegetables at a high temperature to drive out gases that can cause sour tastes and smells.

boiler scale   Chalklike substance that is produced by hard water and that forms hard crusts that can clog hot-water boilers and pipes.

boiling point   Temperature at which the vapor pressure of the liquid is equal to the atmospheric pressure.

brine   Concentrated solution of sodium chloride.

buoyant force   Upward force that a liquid exerts on an object; force is equal to the weight of the liquid that is pushed aside when the object enters the liquid.

calcification   Deposition and growth of calcium crystals.

calorie   Common unit of measuring energy.

Calorie, food   (Spelled with a capital *C* to distinguish from a gram calorie.) Amount of heat needed to increase the temperature of 1,000 grams of water one degree Celsius.

calorie, gram   (Spelled with a lowercase *c* to distinguish from a food Calorie.) Amount of heat energy required to raise the temperature of one gram of water one degree Celsius.

223

calorimeter Instrument that measures the energy released when food burns.

capillary action Rising of the surface of a liquid in small tubes.

catalyst Chemical that changes the rate of a chemical reaction without being changed itself.

cathode Conductor connected to, or the negative terminal of, a battery.

cation Positive chemical particle.

cellobiase Enzyme specific for cellulose.

cellulose Macromolecule made from linking hundreds to thousands of glucose molecules together; found in cell walls of plants.

chemoreceptors Sensory nerves.

chromatogram Color pattern produced on a paper strip during chromatography.

chromatography Method of separating mixtures by encouraging different parts of the mixture to move through an adsorbing material at different rates.

circumference Distance around a circle.

coagulate When molecules come together or clump.

cohesion Force of attraction between like molecules.

collagen Strong fibers of protein.

colligative properties Properties that depend only on the number of particles dissolved in a solvent and not on the nature of the solute or solvent.

colloidal mixture Suspension with large particles permanently dispersed throughout the solvent.

colorfastness Ability of a dye to resist fading.

condensation Change of a vapor into a liquid with a loss of energy.

contract Move closer together.

corrosion Erosion and disintegration of a material.

crystals Solids bound by flat surfaces evenly and regularly arranged.

decant Pour off a liquid from a mixture.

dehydroascorbic acid Acid made by combining vitamin C (ascorbic acid) with iodine; ineffective as a vitamin.

deliquescent Materials that dissolve in the water they absorb from the atmosphere.

denaturing Changing of long chains of protein molecules into smaller separate molecules; changing of the size or shape of protein molecules.

density A mass per unit volume of a material; commonly measured in grams per milliliter (cubic centimeter).

dew Water that condenses on cool surfaces.

dew point Temperature to which air must be cooled, at constant pressure, in order for it to be saturated with water.

diffusion   Self-spreading of molecules from one place to another.
direct dyeing   Method by which dye is affixed directly to cloth.
disaccharide   Complex sugar molecule formed by the combination of two smaller sugar molecules; an example is sucrose.
displace   Push aside or remove out of position.
dissipate   Separate or break up.
elasticity   Ability to return to an original shape after being stretched.
electric current   Flow of electric charges.
electrolysis   Process by which an electric current is used to cause a chemical change.
electrolyte   Substance that conducts an electric current in solution or in a molten state.
energy   Ability to do work.
enzymes   Chemicals that change the rate of a reaction in living organisms but do not change themselves.
equivalents   Quantities of substances that have the same combining capacity.
evaporation   Change of a liquid into a vapor with a gain of energy.
expand   Move farther apart.
extracellular fluid   Fluid outside the cell membrane.
filtrate   Liquid passing through filter paper.
fluid   Material such as a gas or a liquid that is able to flow.
fluidity   Ability to flow.
freezing   Physical change of a liquid to a solid; energy is lost in the change.
freezing point   Temperature at which liquids physically change to a solid.
frost   Covering of ice that forms when water vapor changes directly into a solid at cold temperatures.
gelling   The formation of a jellylike material from a colloidal solution.
hardness of water   Measure of the amount of calcium, magnesium, and/ or iron salts dissolved in water.
heat   Combined energy of all the molecules in a substance.
humidity   Amount of moisture in the atmosphere.
hydrated   Chemical form of a substance with loosely held water molecules.
hydrometer   Instrument used to measure the density of a liquid.
hydrogen ion H^+; present in acidic solutions.
hydroxide ion OH^-; present in basic solutions.
hygrometer   Instrument used to measure humidity.
hygroscopic   Materials that absorb water from the atmosphere.
indicator, acid/base   Dye that changes color in the presence of an acid or a base.
indirect dyeing   Method by which dye unites with a mordant.

inert gases   Gases that either are unable to enter into a chemical reaction or react very slowly.

iodide   Charged particles of iodine; I⁻.

ionic conduction   Electric current produced by the movement of ions in a solution.

ions   Charged particles in a solution.

insulator   Material that restricts or retards heat flow.

kindling temperature   Minimum temperature necessary for a substance to start burning.

kinetic energy   Energy of motion.

matrix   A pattern.

metallic conduction   Electric current produced by a flow of electrons in metal.

micelles, colloidal   Submicroscopic clumps of material ranging in diameter from 3.94×10^{-8} inch (1×10^{-7} cm) to 3.94×10^{-5} inch (1×10^{-4} cm); particles distributed throughout a colloid.

monomers   Small, single molecules linked together to form a large molecule, or polymer.

monosaccharide   Simple, single molecule of sugar; examples are fructose and glucose.

mordant   Substance affixed to the surface of a cloth to which dyes unite.

neutral   Solution with a pH of 7; contains no free hydrogen or hydroxide ions; not acidic or basic.

normality   Number of equivalents of solute per liter of solution.

olfaction   Sense of smell.

osmosis   Movement of water through cell membranes from higher to lower amounts of water.

osmotic pressure   The movement of water through a membrane permeable only to water.

oxidation   Traditional definition is the combination with oxygen; also the loss of electrons in a chemical reaction.

pectin   Gluey material that binds vegetable fibers together.

phases of matter   Gas, liquid, and solid; also called the *physical states* of matter. *Phase changes* occur whenever the physical state of a substance changes.

physical phases   Forms in which matter can be found: gas, liquid, or solid.

pi   math value equaling 3.14.

polar molecules   Molecules having a negative and a positive charge on either side.

polymer   Large molecule composed of many separate molecules bonded together in a chainlike fashion.

polymerization Process of joining small molecules to form a large molecule.

polysaccharide Macromolecule consisting of many sugar molecules linked together; an example is starch.

precipitate Insoluble molecules that separate from a solution.

proteins Large molecules composed of chains of smaller molecules; a nutrient needed for growth and repair of the human body.

redox Term used to represent an oxidation-reduction reaction; a chemical reaction involving exchange of electrons.

reducing agent Chemical that causes other chemicals to gain electrons.

relative humidity Measurement of how much water the air holds at a given temperature.

residue Insoluble solid separated from a mixture; collected by filter paper.

respiration Biochemical reaction by which food combines with oxygen producing carbon dioxide, water, and energy.

reverse calcification Removing the calcium compounds from bones.

rusting Commonly thought of as the combination of iron with oxygen forming a reddish powder; slow oxidation process.

saturated oil Molecules of oil with single bonds between the carbon atoms.

scientific method Technique of scientifically finding answers through the steps of the purpose, hypothesis, research, experimentation, and conclusion.

sizing Material used to fill the pores of fibers of fabric.

soap scum/curd Insoluble salts formed when soap combines with minerals in hard water.

soft water Water without calcium, magnesium, and/or iron cations.

solute Substance dissolved in a solution.

solution Mixture of a solvent and a solute.

solvent Dissolving medium in a solution.

specific dynamic action (SDA) Digesting and metabolizing of food in the human body and converting it into energy.

specific heat Energy required to raise the temperature of one gram of matter one degree Celsius.

stalactite Crystalline deposit hanging from the ceiling of a cave.

stalagmite Crystalline formation growing up from the floor of a cave.

sublimation Direct, reversible change from the gaseous phase to the solid phase.

sugaring Formation of sugar crystals from a saturated solution.

supersaturated Solution that contains a higher concentration of solute than does the saturated solution at a lower temperature.

surface tension   Skinlike film over the surface of liquid created by the strong attraction between the surface molecules.

synthesis   Formation of complex molecules from simpler molecules.

thermodynamics   Study of the movement of energy; from the Greek word *thermos,* which means "heat," and dynamics, which implies movement.

thermometer   Instrument used to measure the average kinetic energy (energy of motion) of molecules.

titration   Combination of a measured amount of a solution of known concentration with a measured amount of solution of unknown concentration.

translational energy   Energy associated with gas molecules as they move linearly from one point to another.

Tyndall effect   Test used to distinguish between a colloid and a pure solution; colloidal particles scatter light and pure solutions do not.

unsaturated oil   Molecules of oil with two or more double bonds between the carbon atoms.

vacuum   Void of matter; empty space.

viscosity   Measurement of thickness of a fluid; resistance to flow.

viscosity index   Viscosity of a fluid relative to the viscosity of water.

vulcanized   Chemical treatment that increases the strength, hardness, and elasticity of rubber; usually involves the addition of sulfur.

water of hydration   Water loosely held by hydrated crystals.

Index

Get these fun and exciting books by Janice VanCleave
at your local bookstore, call toll-free 1-800-225-5945, or fill out the order form below and mail to:
Molly Chesney, John Wiley & Sons, Inc., 605 Third Ave., NY, NY 10158

Janice VanCleave's Science For Every Kid Series

___ Astronomy	53573-7	$11.95 US / 15.95 CAN
___ Biology	50381-9	$11.95 US / 15.95 CAN
___ Chemistry	62085-8	$11.95 US / 15.95 CAN
___ Dinosaurs	30812-9	$11.95 US / 15.95 CAN
___ Earth Science	53010-7	$11.95 US / 15.95 CAN
___ Ecology	10086-2	$11.95 US / 15.95 CAN
___ Geography	59842-9	$11.95 US / 15.95 CAN
___ Geometry	31141-3	$11.95 US / 15.95 CAN
___ Human Body	02408-2	$11.95 US / 15.95 CAN
___ Math	54265-2	$11.95 US / 15.95 CAN
___ Oceans	12453-2	$11.95 US / 15.95 CAN
___ Physics	52505-7	$11.95 US / 15.95 CAN

over 1 million VanCleave books sold

Janice VanCleave's Spectacular Science Projects

___ Animals	55052-3	$10.95 US / 12.95 CAN
___ Earthquakes	57107-5	$10.95 US / 12.95 CAN
___ Electricity	31010-7	$10.95 US / 12.95 CAN
___ Gravity	55050-7	$10.95 US / 12.95 CAN
___ Machines	57108-3	$10.95 US / 12.95 CAN
___ Magnets	57106-7	$10.95 US / 12.95 CAN
___ Microscopes & Magnifying Lenses	58956-X	$10.95 US / 12.95 CAN
___ Molecules	55054-X	$10.95 US / 12.95 CAN
___ Rocks and Minerals	10269-5	$10.95 US / 12.95 CAN
___ Volcanoes	30811-0	$10.95 US / 12.95 CAN
___ Weather	03231-X	$10.95 US / 12.95 CAN

Janice VanCleave's Science Bonanzas

___ 200 Gooey, Slippery, Slimy, Weird & Fun Experiments	57921-1	$12.95 US / 16.95 CAN
___ 201 Awesome, Magical, Bizarre & Incredible Experiments	31011-5	$12.95 US / 16.95 CAN
___ 202 Oozing, Bubbling, Dripping & Bouncing Experiments	14025-2	$12.95 US / 16.95 CAN

Janice VanCleave's A+ Projects

___ Biology	58628-5	$12.95 US / 17.95 CAN
___ Chemistry	58630-7	$12.95 US / 17.95 CAN

[ ] Check/Money order enclosed
(Wiley pays shipping. Please include $2.50 for handling charges.)
[ ] Charge my: [ ]VISA   [ ]MASTERCARD   [ ]AMEX   [ ]DISCOVER
Card #:_____ Expiration Date:_____/_____
NAME:_____
ADDRESS:_____
CITY/STATE/ZIP:_____
SIGNATURE:_____

(Order not valid unless signed)

WILEY
Publishers Since 1807